Be Perfect as Your Heavenly Father

Be Perfect as Your Heavenly Father

God is calling you to a life of Perfection

Isaac Idemudia

LIBRARY OF CONGRESS CONTROL NUMBER: 2014906976
ISBN: HARDCOVER   978-1-4990-0249-2
             SOFTCOVER   978-1-4990-0251-5
             EBOOK   978-1-4990-0243-0

Scripture quotations, unless otherwise noted, have been taken from the King James Version of the Bible.

Scripture quotations marked NASB are taken from the New American Standard Bible. © 1960, 1962, 1963, 1968, 1971, 1972, 1973, 1975, 1977, 1995 by the Lockman Foundation.
Used with permission. (www.Lockman.org)

Scripture quotations marked AMP are taken from the Amplified® Bible. © 1954, 1958, 1962, 1964, 1965, 1987 by the Lockman Foundation.
Used with permission. (www.Lockman.org)

This book was printed in the United States of America.

Rev. date: 05/02/2014

Books also available in: Amazon, Barnes & Nobles, Borders and also in ebook format.

To order additional copies of this book, contact:
Xlibris LLC
1-888-795-4274
www.Xlibris.com
Orders@Xlibris.com
550329

and

Good Shepherd Christian Ministries
Email: *gscm7@yahoo.com*
Website: www.gscministries.org

CONTENTS

Acknowledgments.. 11

Introduction... 13

Chapter 1 Who Am I?.. 17

Chapter 2 Walking in Dominion........................... 36

Chapter 3 Living in Obedience to God.................. 59

Chapter 4 Forgiveness.. 79

Chapter 5 Message for God's Servants 89

Chapter 6 Holiness... 99

Chapter 7 Be Perfect 117

This book is dedicated to the Most High God.

"Be Perfect As Your heavenly Father." What boldness and insight God gave Pastor Isaac Idemudia to write on a topic that many in the Body of Christ think is impossible to attain unto. Perfection is God's Master Plan for His children as we see documented in the scriptures, and Pastor Idemudia has done well by taking the time to expound on this simple and yet profound topic. Whether you are just starting your journey in the faith, or you have been running the race for a while, I strongly recommend you read this book."

Pastor Gideon Daspan
RCCG—Empowerment Center
Kalamazoo, Michigan USA

"This book is an important, timely word for believers and seekers. It is a clear, insightful, and inspiring call to the Life of God that is in Christ Jesus our Lord."

Bob Beaver
Pastor, Christian Church of San Angelo
San Angelo, Texas USA

Acknowledgments

I would like to acknowledge my Heavenly Father, the Alpha and the Omega, the first and the last; without His redemptive plan for me, I would have been lost. My acknowledgment also goes to my Lord and Savior Jesus Christ, the author and finisher of my faith, the bright and morning star, and the shepherd of my soul. He paid for my sins that I may live an everlasting life with God the Father in heaven. I acknowledge the ever-present and gentle Holy Spirit, my teacher and comforter; the one who guides me daily and reveals the deep things of God. I give God all the glory and honor.

I thank my beautiful wife, Francisca, for her love, devotion, and ceaseless support for the call of God in my life. You are a blessing not only to our children and me but also to the body of Christ. I love you dearly.

To my children, you are a blessing from the Lord, and you all have been my biggest cheerleaders during the course of my writing this book. I love you all.

My appreciation goes out to the special people in my life who contributed to the editing and proofreading of this book. Your reward is eternal, in Jesus name.

Introduction

Just as an infant learns to walk and a supermodel masters the catwalk, so must a Christian learn to walk perfectly with God. This is not a choice but a requirement for all believing Christians that love the Lord. If you sincerely love the Lord, you will obey him. The word *Christian* simply means "a follower of Christ." If we are to carry that emblem, we must be true followers of Christ and not by name only. The world judges by the outward appearance of man, but God looks at our hearts, and you cannot manipulate or swindle Him. If we are charged in court for being a Christian, would there be enough evidence to convict us without any doubt? Do you have one foot in the world and one foot in the kingdom of God? Though we live in this world, we are certainly not part of this world. Jesus Christ spoke to the Pharisees and scribes in Matthew 23:23 saying, "Woe to you, Scribes and Pharisees, hypocrites! For you pay tithe of mint and anise and cumin, and have neglected the weightier matters of the law." In other words, it is not enough to say I pay my tithe and attend church regularly and think my walk with God is complete. Jesus went further to explain in Matthew 23:23 saying, "These you ought to have done, without leaving the others undone." This means, yes, you are expected to pay your tithe and offering, but that is not the end of your walk with God. Bringing our tithes and offerings into God's house is a scriptural injunction, but God is much more interested in our walk with Him, as we saw in the life of Enoch (Genesis 5:24). Our Heavenly Father craves for a personal relationship with us, knowing fully well that our earthly currencies that are not being spent in heaven cannot suffice for our place in His heart. Jesus only mentioned a few of the weightier matters such as justice, mercy, and faith, but to perfect one's walk with Him is also a requirement for believers; otherwise, he would not have commanded us in Matthew 5:48 (KJV) when He said, "Be ye therefore perfect, even as your Father which is in Heaven is perfect." If you are to be called followers of Christ, then you must allow the Holy Spirit to perfect your walk with Christ. This is the premise upon which the Holy Spirit inspired me to write this book. It is not written to condemn you but to wake believers who are in spiritual slumber. We need to be alert for we know not when the master will come like a thief in the night. Over the years in my walk with the

Lord, I have learned to depend upon the Lord to complete His work in my life. As you read this book, may the Holy Spirit complete His perfect work in your life in Jesus Christ's name.

Chapter 1

WHO AM I?

Many have attempted to define and answer the age-old questions "who am I?" and "what's my purpose on earth?" These are questions that every human on earth should have answers to. We all need to find out who we are because if we don't know who we are, people will define us. The issue of self-identity cannot be overemphasized (John 1:21-23). A lot of people are being misguided and misled simply because they don't know who they are. The full understanding of self-identity is what determines your level of dominion, command, mastery, and inheritance (Psalm 82:6, John 10:34).

The fact is we are created by God and for a purpose. The Bible tells us in Genesis 1:26 that God created us different from the animals. We are not created like other living things. Our creation was intentionally designed by God to be different from His other creations. When it came to the creation of man, God deliberately created man in His image and according to His likeness. *Merriam-Webster* defines *image* as "a visual representation of something." This tells me that God created me in His likeness as His visual representation here on earth.

So before we identify who we are and why we were created, we must first identify who God is and why He created us different from His other creations. Why did our God take such an interest in creating us in His image and likeness?

> *And God said, Let us make man in our image, after our likeness: and let them have dominion over the fish of the sea, and over the fowl of the air, and over the cattle, and over all the earth, and over every creeping thing that creepeth upon the earth.*
>
> —Genesis 1:26

WHO IS GOD?

God is a supreme being, the eternal creator. He is the ruler of heaven and earth. We are told in John 1:1-5 that God existed in the beginning, and the Bible calls Him the Alpha and the Omega—the first and the last—because He is the initiator of all things and concludes all things. There was nothing made that was made without Him.

In the beginning was the Word, and the Word was with God, and the Word was God.

The same was in the beginning with God.

All things were made by him; and without him was not anything made that was made.

In him was life; and the life was the light of men.

And the light shineth in darkness; and the darkness comprehended it not.

—John 1:1-5 (KJV)

Genesis 14:18 describes him as Jehovah Elyon, God Most High. This name reveals God's exalted nature. He is the King of Glory (Psalm 24:10), and the High and Lifted One (Isaiah 6:1). He is Jehovah Adonai, our sovereign God (Acts 4:24), and Isaiah 9:6 describes Him as El Gibbor, the Mighty God, the one that is strong and mighty in battle.

God is a Spirit and God is one, but He exists in three persons: God the Father, God the Son, and God the Holy Spirit.

God is a Spirit and they that worship him must worship him in Spirit and in truth.

—John 4:24 (KJV)

So we have God the Father, who is the first person in the Godhead, and we have God the Son and God the Spirit, and together they are one God. The Bible declares in 1 John 5:7, "For there are three that bear record in heaven, the Father, the Word and the Holy Ghost: and these three are one." And the *Word* is Jesus Christ.

What Is the Divine Nature of God?

Omnipotent

God is omnipotent, which means He is all-powerful. There is no one that compares with Him. He has power to create and power to destroy. He answers to no one and takes no counsel from any man. Matthew 19:26 states that "with God all things are possible." And also in Jeremiah 32:27, God stated, "Behold, I am the Lord, the God of all flesh: is there anything too hard for me?"

Omnipresent

God is omnipresent, which means he is present everywhere. We cannot hide from Him. If we hide deep inside the cave, He is there. If we hide in the depths of the sea, He is also there. If we try to hide in the planet above, He is there. God has the ability to be present everywhere at the same time. Ezekiel 48:35 describes Him as Jehovah

Shammah, the Lord is Present. Psalm 139:7 states, "Whither shall I go from thy Spirit? Or whither shall I flee from thy presence?" We cannot flee from God's presence or hide from Him. He sees and watches everything we do and knows the thoughts of our hearts.

OMNISCIENT

God is omniscient, which means all-knowing. He knew us before we were born; He knows us now and knows what decision we will make in the next minute. So God knows everything in the past, present, and future. His knowledge is infinite. Psalm 147:5 states, "Great is our Lord, and of great power: His understanding is infinite."

It's quite unfortunate that humans cannot completely or fully describe who God is. How can a limited being begin to fully understand a limitless God? The Bible states in 1 Corinthians 13:9-10, "For we know in part, and we prophesy in part. But when that which is perfect is come, then that which is in part shall be done away." Our God is beyond description and human comprehension because He alone is God, and there will never be any like Him.

WHAT IS THE CHARACTER OF GOD?

Let us try to explore who God is by examining some of His attributes.

1. LOVE

God is love (1 John 4:8 NASB). The Bible tells us in John 3:16 that "for God so loved the world, that He gave His only begotten Son, that whosoever believeth in Him should not perish, but have everlasting life." Starting from Creation, God loved man even when man disobeyed God. His love was never based on any condition. The love of God is best described in 1 Corinthians 13:4-7 (NASB), which states, "Love is patient, it is kind and not jealous; love does not brag and is not arrogant, does not act unbecomingly; it does not seek its own, is not provoked, does not take into account a wrong suffered, does not rejoice in unrighteousness, but rejoices with the truth; bears all things, believes all things, hope all things, endures all things." God loves even the heinous criminal alive, and He takes no pleasure in the death of anyone, including the wicked (Ezekiel 18:32).

2. MERCY

God is merciful (Deuteronomy 4:31). Using the synonyms for *merciful,* we can say God is compassionate, kindhearted, lenient, generous, sympathetic, forgiving, and gracious. The Bible tells us in Psalm 103:8 that "the Lord is merciful and gracious, slow to anger, and plenteous in mercy."

3. SUPREME

God is supreme and he is above all. He is self-existing and self-governing. The Bible tells us in Colossians 1:16-17 (NASB), "For by Him all things were created, both in the heavens and on the earth, visible and invisible, whether thrones or dominions or rulers or authorities—all things have been created through Him and for Him. He is before all things and in Him all things hold together."

4. ETERNAL

God is eternal and never-ending. He lives and reigns forever and ever. Luke 1:33 describes the eternal reign of God: "And he shall reign over the house of Jacob forever; and of his kingdom there shall be no end."

5. IMMUTABLE

God is immutable, which means "not subject to change." He is unchangeable and unmovable. The Bible says in Hebrews 13:8 that "Jesus Christ the same yesterday, and to day, and for ever."

6. PERFECT

God is perfect, and there is no error in Him. Everything about God is excellent. Psalm 18:30 states, "As for God his way is perfect: the word of God is tried: he is a buckler to all those that trust in him."

7. JUST

God is just; there is no favoritism attached to Him. He will treat you fairly and judge you fairly. 2 Thessalonians 1:6 (NASB) states, "For after all it is only just for God to repay with affliction those who afflict you."

8. TRUSTWORTHY

God is trustworthy. We can depend on Him to do what He said He will do. He will never lie. Numbers 23:19 explains the trustworthiness of God. It states, "God is not a man, that he should lie; neither the son of man, that he should repent: hath he said, and shall he not do it? or hath he spoken, and shall he not make it good?"

9. HOLY

God is holy; He cannot sin nor partake of anything called sin. His eyes cannot behold iniquity. Revelation 15:4 says, "Who shall not fear thee, O Lord, and glorify thy name? for thou only art holy: for all nations shall come and worship before thee; for thy judgments are made manifest."

1O. FAITHFUL

God is faithful; He is faithful to His promises. He has never failed and will never fail. He promised Abraham a son, and it came to pass. He is a God that does not break covenants. He honors His words. Deuteronomy 7:9 states, "Know therefore that the Lord thy God, He is God, the faithful God, which keepeth covenant and mercy with them that love him and keep his commandments to a thousand generations."

WHY DID GOD CREATE US IN HIS OWN IMAGE AND LIKENESS?

Why will God bother to create man when there are numerable hosts of angels to worship and serve Him in heaven? One thing we know is that God does not live on American dollars; neither does He spend any currency on earth for the gold and silver are His (Haggai 2:8). He does not feed on food, although He owns all the animals and food crops in the world. One thing God feeds on is praise. He created man for His own pleasure so as to receive glory and honor and praise from man, not to send man to hell. Hell was never originally created for man, but man found a way to send himself there through disobedience.

> *Thou art worthy, O Lord, to receive glory and honour and power: for thou hast created all things, and for thy pleasure they are and were created.*
> —Revelation 4:11

Once man was created, God instantly loved man and created a companion for him. He gave man dominion over all His other creations until man disobeyed and gave his authority to satan. Because of the love God has for man, He quickly assigned an angel in the entrance to the garden with a flaming sword that turned every way to keep Adam from the tree of life (Genesis 3:22-24). This action of love from God kept Adam from living perpetually separated from God in sin. The Bible states, "But God commendeth his love toward us, in that, while we were yet sinners, Christ died for us" (Romans 5:8).

With the love for man still burning in God's heart, He provided a sacrificial lamb in the person of His only begotten son to come to earth and atone once and for all the sins of mankind, that whosoever believes in the Lord Jesus Christ and the work He did on the cross would be saved.

So I humbly submit that the purpose of man's creation was to bring God pleasure (Revelation 4:11).

WAYS WE CAN PLEASE GOD

1. FAITH

One way we can please God and bring him pleasure is by having faith in Him. The Bible tells us in Hebrews 11:6 that "but without faith it is impossible to please him: for he that cometh to God must believe that he is, and that he is a rewarder of them that diligently seek him."

2. PRAISE

Through praise, we can bring honor and glory to God (Malachi 2:1-2, Psalm 92:1, Psalm 100:1-5, Psalm 103:1). He dwells in our praise, and the angels in heaven worship Him continually. The Bible states in Psalm 22:3, "But thou art holy, O thou that inhabitest the praise of Israel."

King David lived to please God. He knew how to praise and worship God. He found favor in the sight of God, and God called him a man after his own heart.

3. THE FEAR OF GOD

The fear of God will cause one to shun evil. As born-again believers, we no longer own ourselves because we have been bought with the precious blood of Jesus (1 Corinthians 6:20). God was so pleased with Job's perfect walk with Him that he bragged about Job to satan (Job 1: 6-8). There are few things the Lord demands from us; one of them is having the fear of the Lord. Deuteronomy 10:12-13 (NASB) states, "Now, Israel, what does the Lord your God require from you, but to fear the Lord your God, to work in all his ways and Love Him, and to serve the Lord your God with all your heart and with all your soul, and to keep the Lord's commandments and His statutes which I am commanding you today for your good?"

4. Obedience

God does not take delight in our disobedience; rather, He takes pleasure in our obedience. 1 Samuel 15:22-23 reads, "And Samuel said, Hath the Lord as great delight in burnt offerings and sacrifices, as in obeying the voice of the Lord? Behold, to obey is better than sacrifice, and to hearken than the fat of rams." When our obedience is complete, God is pleased and rewards us with His covenant blessings. The bible says in Job 36:11 "If they obey and serve him, they shall spend their days in prosperity, and their years in pleasure." So another way we can bring God pleasure is to surrender our life to Him and obey His commandments. Choosing to live our lives on our own terms and conditions does not bring God pleasure. May you decide today to live your life to please Him.

You Are a Spirit Being

One of the ways to further prove the indescribability of God is the potency of His triune nature. 1 John 5:7 validated this truth. The Godhead expresses Himself in three personalities that are inseparable. However, because every born-again child of God has *the very life of God transmitted into him or her via new birth and the infilling of the Holy Ghost, man has a triune nature as well. Man is a spirit; he has a soul and lives in a* body. So the triune nature of man is spirit, soul, and body. At birth, our spirit, which was birthed in sin, was very carnal and not regenerated. In this state, man is unable to connect with God and will remain eternally separated from God unless his spirit is regenerated or born again. That is why God communicates not to our flesh but to our spirit. God is not made of flesh and blood, but He is a Spirit, and it is in the image of His spirit that you were created. As unbelievers, that spirit is dead in sin and eternally separated from God. So it is through our spiritual rebirth in Jesus Christ that we are able to be reconciled to the Father.

> *The spirit of man is the candle of the Lord,*
> *searching all the inward parts of the belly.*
>
> —Proverbs 20:27

Soul

The soul comprises our mind, will, and emotion. At birth, our soul was also very carnal. It thinks carnally and influences the spirit man to act carnally. After our spirit is regenerated or born again, our soul, though aware that the spirit man has been regenerated, still wants to act in its old sinful nature, hence the need for our minds to be retrained or renewed in the ways of the Lord. The call to renew our minds is not a onetime thing but rather a daily transformation of our lives by the continual renewing of our minds.

And be not conformed to this world: but be ye transformed by the renewing of your mind, that ye may prove what is good, and acceptable, and perfect, will of God.

—Romans 12:2

Body

So the real you is your spirit and your flesh is just a vessel called a body that houses your five senses, which are sight, smell, taste, hearing, and touch. When you die, the body returns to dust. The body will always desire to sin and disobey God as long as the spirit man is not regenerated. There is a war between the flesh and the spirit. In Romans

7:15-25, we recollect how painfully Apostle Paul narrated his personal struggle of wanting to do good while still under the law but finding himself doing the evil things he did not want to do. This reiterates the need to walk in the spirit and keep our bodies under subjection.

> *But I keep under my body, and bring it into subjection: lest that by any means, when I have preached to others, I myself should be a castaway.*
> —1 Corinthians 9:27

Do We Reflect God's Attributes?

So if God created us in his image and likeness, why do we not reflect His attributes? Why is everything that is characterized in God not found in us? This might be a good question for you and me to ponder on or a good time to revisit the manner in which we have lived our lives. Jesus did not come to condemn us but to save the lost. Likewise, this book was written not to condemn you but to alert and wake many who are in spiritual slumber. The coming of Christ is closer at hand, and we must be ready like the five wise virgins to meet the bridegroom. The Lord expects you and me as His brides to bring honor to Him just as you would want honor from your children and your parents would want honor from you.

That all men should honour the Son, even as they honour the Father. He that honoureth not the Son honoureth not the Father which hath sent him.

—John 5:23

The Word of God says, "That all should honor the Son." Whom is the Bible referring to? It is evident that God wants everyone to honor Him not with lip service but by living a life of obedience to God. Sure, we are saved by grace through faith in Christ Jesus, but does that mean we now have license to sin or live a life that is dishonoring to God? Certainly not!

WHOSE IMAGE OR LIKENESS DO YOU BEAR?

God created us in His image and likeness, but sin has separated man from God. We are slaves to whom we yield our members. Jesus Christ died for us on the cross to free us from the clutches of sin. Men have turned away from God and now bear the image and likeness of the devil. Just like the Israelites constantly turned from God during their exodus from Egypt. They betrayed His love by turning to idolatry even when they witnessed the miraculous hand of God. They chose rather to reject the protection and provision of God. We are certainly not different from them. We have allowed the pleasures of this world—sex, money, fame, and power—to entice us away from God.

> *They made a calf in Horeb, and worshipped a molten image. Thus they changed their glory into the similitude of an ox that eateth grasss. They forgat God their saviour, which had done great things in Egypt; Wondrous works in the land of Ham, and terrible things by the Red Sea.*
>
> —Psalm 106:19-22

Whose image and likeness do you bear? Is your public life different from your private life? Do you exhibit holier-than-thou attitude in the public and around Christian brethren and then display the real you in private? You can deceive men and live a double life, but you cannot deceive God. He looks at our hearts and knows our motives. We are to live our lives as an epistle of God. Our *yes* must be yes, and our *no* must be no. When we say something is white, it must be white. Do not act or say one thing in public and do another in private. If we say we have the image and likeness of God, then we must live our lives to be more like Christ daily and not allow the evil world to defile us. We serve a God that changes not. He is the same yesterday, today, and forever. God loves you, and He is willing today to transform you to His image and likeness if you so desire.

So Who Are You?

These are some of your identities in Christ as a born-again believer in Christ Jesus:

You are the righteousness of Christ (2 Corinthians 5:21).

You are co-heir with Christ (Romans 8:17).

You are more than conqueror (Romans 8:37).

You are the light of the world (Matthew 5:14).

You are salt of the earth (Matthew 5:13).

You are the head not the tail (Deuteronomy 28:13).

You are above not beneath (Deuteronomy 28:13).

You have the mind of Christ (1 Corinthians 2:16).

You seated with Christ in the heavenly places (Ephesians 2:6).

As Christ is so are you (1 John 4:17).

You are god (John 10:34).

You are blessed (Psalm 115:15).

You are loved by God (John 3:16).

You are the redeemed of the Lord (Psalm 107:2).

You are sanctified and justified (1 Corinthians 6:11).

You are the apple of God's eye (Zachariah 2:8).

You are crowned with honor and glory (Psalm 8:5).

Do not allow the enemy or anyone to define you, and do not sell your birthright to satan as Adam and Eve did for a piece of fruit. Jesus paid for your new identity, so walk in it.

Chapter 2

WALKING IN DOMINION

DOMINION

In Genesis, God changed a situation that was void and without form, where only darkness reigned supreme, and turned it into a place with form, full of life and light. He personally planted a beautiful garden for Adam and Eve, and all they had to do was tend to the garden and lift up their fingers to eat. The garden was green and lush with flowing rivers full of abundant food source. It was a very beautiful garden, and God was pleased with it. The first and most important blessing God bestowed on man was that of dominion over His creation on earth. Dominion means having power, authority, command, control, or having dominance over something or territory (Genesis 1:26-28).

When God created us, He gave us control over His creation on earth. But man willingly gave it up to the devil through disobedience to God. Christ then has to come to

reclaim what was lost in order to bring us to our rightful place with God the Father. We are now seated with Christ in the heavenly places far above principalities and power.

> *And hath raised us up together, and made us sit together in heavenly places in Christ Jesus.*
> —Ephesians 2:6

We are created to be conquerors, victors, winners, and to dominate any challenges the enemy may bring our way. 2 Corinthians 4:8-9 states, "We are troubled on every side, yet not distressed; we are perplexed but not in despair; Persecuted, but not forsaken; cast down, but not destroyed." And it concluded in verse 17 saying that "for our light affliction, which is but for a moment, worketh for us a far more exceeding and eternal weight of glory." Praise God!

You may be facing challenges of poverty, failure, sickness, or challenges in your business or relationship, and you might be struggling with carnal thoughts, pornography, immorality, smoking, alcoholism, anger, or bitterness, or be plagued with the spirit of deceit, but the Lord is able to deliver you from it all. As long as the Lord lives, you can never remain cast down and perplexed. That light affliction is just for a moment, and I command every affliction in your life to end now in Jesus name.

There was a time in my life when I struggled with a particular sin. I know I ought not to do it, but I found myself falling again and again into this particular sin. I was like a sheep led to the slaughter—just as Paul spoke about in Romans 7:18-25, stating the struggle he had with his flesh, which is similar to the struggle many believers are facing today or are secretly going through. But my deliverance came one night when I cried out to the Lord and asked the Holy Spirit to come to deliver me. That was the end of my struggle, and I completely lost the taste for sin, and my only desire in life now is to please the Lord in words, thoughts, and deeds. May the Spirit of God break every yoke of sin in your life, and may you hate sin and lose the taste for it in Jesus name.

In Mark 10:46-52, blind Bartimaeus was told to stop crying for Jesus. They said to him, "Hold your peace." In other words, "Manage your blindness and be content with it and do not bother Jesus." But Bartimaeus cried out the more to Jesus, and Jesus stopped and healed him. Until you reach your desperation point and want no more of that sin, you will not get your deliverance. The Bible states, in Matthew 11:12, "And from the days of John the Baptist until now the kingdom of heaven suffereth violence, and the violent take it by force." I do not know what struggle you are going through or what sin is plaguing you, but until you become

violent in your Spirit and say "enough is enough," you will continue to struggle with that sin or affliction. I break every stronghold in your life in the mighty name of Jesus Christ.

In Matthew 21:12-13, Jesus did not put up with the money changers who turned the house of God into a den of thieves. Likewise, you must evict every demonic spirit that has turned your body, which is the temple of God, into a den of thieves where all form of evil is being permeated. Cry to Jesus today, and He will set you free.

You are born to be the head and not the tail, to be above and not beneath (Deuteronomy 28:13). Why then are some believers in Jesus Christ still having victim mentality? Your friends or loved ones may abandon you, and they may tell you to abandon your faith in God. But be assured that our God is aware of your situation, and just like Job (Job 42:10), He wants to deliver and restore you—but you must first be willing to be delivered. In Matthew 9:12, Jesus said that He came for only those that are sick and need physicians, so until you accept that you are sick and need Jesus, you are not a candidate for healing. Jesus is willing to turn every oppressive situation that you are going through to a victorious walk with Him. The Bible says in Obadiah 1:17, "But upon mount Zion shall be deliverance, and there shall be holiness; and the house of Jacob shall possess their possessions." Be delivered from every demonic stronghold in your life in the mighty name of Jesus, and you shall possess your possessions in Jesus mighty name. Know that the Lord does not take pleasure in your downfall; rather, it pleases Him when you are prospering physically and spiritually.

Exercise Your Authority

God is sovereign, meaning He exercises authority and reigns. Do you have authority and reign like your Heavenly Father, or is the evil one having a field day with you? May that not be your portion? Arise and take your throne. Fear not for the evil one is a defeated foe. The authority of God came to play when Jesus healed a man that was demon-possessed. The scripture described it perfectly in Mark 5:7-8. When one of the demons that possessed the man saw Jesus, he cried out in a loud voice saying, "What have I to do with thee, Jesus, thou Son of the most high God? I adjure thee by God, that thou torment me not." The demons inside the man were quivering in terror because the master had arrived, and they were uncertain what fate awaited them. So they did what they do not practice; that is, they begged for mercy. They knew the man with authority was here, and it was time to beg for mercy. The Bible recorded that the demons pleaded with Jesus not to be tormented but to be sent into the swine. It is amazing to me how the demons begged not to be tormented when they were the ones tormenting this man for probably many years. Don't we serve a merciful and long-suffering God? Even when He had the opportunity to deal mercilessly with the demons, He chose rather to restrain His power and send them to the swine knowing that their day of reckoning was certainly coming.

How about you? Do demons tremble when you show up on the scene, or do you tremble when you encounter them? When you are placed in a position of authority, do you deal mercilessly or skillfully manipulate your way to fulfill your desires? These are the questions you have to answer for yourself. You need not be afraid of the evil one for he is a defeated foe. The work of defeating him is already done on the cross, and it is up to you to make sure he remains defeated in your life. Do not give him any foothold into your affairs. You are the one with authority and power. Don't be intimated.

Paul was not afraid to use his power in Christ Jesus. He boldly used that power to heal the sick, and he worked unusual miracles. The Jewish exorcist attempted to cast out demons from those that were possessed just as Paul did. Rather, they were dealt with by the demons.

> *And the evil spirit answered and said, Jesus I know, and Paul I know; but who are ye?*
>
> —Acts 19:15

Are you relevant and on fire for Jesus to be noticed by demons? Start exercising the authority you have in Christ Jesus.

Jesus calmed the fierce storm that brought about high winds and waves capable of capsizing a boat. The disciples reacted like most average Christians would by panicking and getting very anxious. They were moved by their sight; what they saw led them to react in fear, and that is how the enemy wants you to operate on a daily basis. Once the enemy succeeds in creating fear, you are bound to make irrational decisions.

The disciples, out of fear, woke up Jesus to rescue them. Jesus responded by rebuking them and questioning their faith. Likewise, when we are in Christ Jesus and going through challenges in life, we should not be moved by sight but by the Word of God. Am not one that get irritated easily but one thing that gets under my skin is when we as believers take it upon ourselves to question the fairness of God when we are going through challenges in life. What an audacity to question the ways of God. Are we wiser than God? We must learn to bless the name of the Lord at all times through good and challenging times. We must not allow our circumstance to dictate how we relate to God. We are not fair-weather Christians who only love God when things are going well. We should have confidence in the God we serve.

WE ARE MORE THAN CONQUERORS

We are not created to be victims, but to be victors. Until you know who you are as a conqueror, you will not have command over God's creations. That is why Paul explained in Romans 8:37, "Nay, in all these things we are more than conquerors through him that loved us." We are conquerors not just in certain area of our lives but in all areas. In our spiritual lives, we are more than conquerors; in our careers, businesses or marital lives, we are more than conquerors.

To conquer is to overcome, to defeat or triumph over any challenges in your life. As a born again believer, Jesus took away your sin, infirmities, poverty—your burdens— and nailed them on the cross. He also broke every yoke of the enemy in your life that had you bound. He literally set you free from bondage and gave you power to continue to triumph over sin, sickness, poverty, and every challenge of life. The Bible said in Isaiah 53:4, "Surely he hath borne our griefs, and carried our sorrows." If Christ took and bore my sins, infirmities, and everything that is causing me grief and sorrow, then I no longer have them. So until you relinquish and cast all your cares and burdens unto the Lord, you will not experience a victorious life as a conqueror.

Are you in a situation where you have no hope, and all you have received from people is hopelessness? Wake up from your pity party and take your place in the kingdom.

You need to get to a point in your life where you become angry in your spirit with the devil and say, "Enough is enough. I will not experience any more lack in my life. No more sickness, no more living a life without Jesus, and no more wallowing in sin." Jesus died for you and me and took away all our sins, sicknesses, lack, and burdens on the cross that you and I may have an abundant life with God. But the devil has come to steal from you, to kill and to destroy every good work in you. The only refuge and protection is in Jesus Christ.

> *The thief cometh not, but for to steal, and to kill,*
> *and to destroy: I am come that they might have life,*
> *and that they might have it more abundantly.*
> —John 10:10

In the tenth chapter of John, Jesus declared that we are gods.

> *Jesus answered them, Is it not written in your*
> *law, I said, Ye are gods?*
> —John 10:34

If we are gods, then God has created us to rule and have dominion on this earth. *The Merriam-Webster Dictionary* defined *god* as a "powerful ruler, a person or thing of supreme value."

You are a powerful ruler. The devil or the prince of this dark world has no power over you. You are sealed by the Holy Spirit and covered in the blood of Jesus. The Bible says we are hidden in Christ Jesus (Colossians 3:3). God the Father no longer sees you as a wicked sinner, but one that has been bought and washed cleaned with the precious blood of the Lamb. The day you gave your life to Jesus, your sin in heaven was wiped clean, never to be remembered again. As the redeemed of the Lord, we now have the power to bind and loose or decree according to the will of God with our lips, and God will honor it in heaven. Do not see yourself as a commoner. We belong to a royal kingdom whose king is the King of Kings.

> *But ye are a chosen generation, a royal priesthood, an holy nation, a peculiar people; that ye should shew forth the praises of him who hath called you out of darkness into his marvelous light.*
>
> —1 Peter 2:9

God has called our generation and generations before us a chosen generation. He has called us to be a royal priesthood and a holy nation. We are not called to live as victims but to live in dominion. The Lord has given us power over all the powers of the enemy (Luke 10:19). Start seeing yourself as God sees you.

God said in 2 Peter 1:3, "According as his divine power hath given unto us all things that pertain unto life and godliness, through the knowledge of him that hath called us to glory and virtue." Everything we need to succeed in life and have dominion has been given to us. No good commander-in-chief will send his soldiers to battle without equipping his men with all the necessary weapons needed to overcome the enemy. Our heavenly Father has not left us as orphans; He has not restrained anything from us. He freely gave us Jesus Christ, and with the name of Jesus, we became more than conquerors. The Bible says in Philippians 2:9-10, "Wherefore God also hath highly exalted him, and given him a name which is above every name: That at the name of Jesus every knee should bow, of things in heaven, and things in earth, and things under the earth."

As believers, God has given us a name we can call in time of trouble or challenges. That name is Jesus Christ. There is nothing in heaven, earth, or under the earth that will not bow to the name of Jesus. At the name of Jesus, all issues representing a mountain in your life will bow. By invoking the name of Jesus, every issue representing Goliath in your life will cease to exist. All principalities and powers, poverty, or sickness will bow at the name of Jesus. This is a name that is above all names and a name that cures any incurable disease known to man. The name of Jesus causes the enemy to tremble and bow.

FACTORS THAT HINDER OUR VICTORIOUS WALK IN DOMINION

1. DISOBEDIENCE

God desires that we win the battle of life and overcome the challenges of life so we can begin to rule and reign. God has given us all things we need to live a godly and victorious life here on earth, and all we have to do is wake up to that realization and begin tapping into the power we have in Christ Jesus.

It is you who is privileged to be created in God's image and likeness, not the angels or the devil; it is you to whom the dominion over God's creation on earth was given, not the devil, so why are some believers acting like a victim and conceding their power and dominion over to the *devil*? When we disobey God and choose rather to do it our way, we are unknowingly surrendering our power and dominion over to the devil.

When we live in a state of disobedience to the commandments of God and refuse to repent, we are conceding our power and dominion to satan, thereby arming him with the authority to put a crack in our spiritual armor. If we do not turn from our wicked ways and repent, then that crack will become a big, gaping hole to your defensive shield that God has placed over you. You unknowingly give the enemy a foothold in your life. As citizens of the kingdom of God, we must put on the full armor of God at all times so we can stand against the wiles of the devil (Ephesians 6:11).

The Bible says in Daniel 11:32b, "But the people that do know their God shall be strong, and do exploits." *Merriam-Webster* defines *exploits* as "a deed, act or to make productive use of." So God has called us to be strong in spirit, body, and soul so we can productively use the authority we have at our disposal. May the Lord open our spiritual eyes to see the great and mighty things He has in store for you and me in Jesus name. May you be the conqueror he has created you to be in Jesus name.

The good news is that the power and authority Adam and Eve conceded to satan has been restored back to us. We are the redeemed of the Lord with restored power and authority in Christ Jesus. We are the victorious people of God.

[The Father] has delivered and drawn us
to Himself out of the control and dominion of

darkness and has transferred us into the kingdom of the Son of His love.

—Colossians 1:13 AMP

2. Our Tongue

Another reason some Christians do not live a victorious life of dominion is because of the misuse of their tongue. God has given us the power and authority to transform our situation. No matter what the situation is, victory is already ours because Jesus has done it on the cross. If you don't like your environment or situation, you change it. How do you do that? Through the creative power that lies in your tongue and by stepping out in faith to accomplish what God has promised you. Numbers 23:19 tells us that God is not a man that He should lie. If He promised it, it shall surely come to pass. He is faithful even when we are clouded with doubts. There is power in your tongue (Proverbs 18:21); whether you believe it or not, it does not take away from the fact that it is true. Your tongue has the power to change your situation and shape your destiny. Saying the wrong word can hurt and cost you in a negative way, and when the tongue is used wisely, it can usher you to your divine blessings.

As Christians, it is wrong for us to use our tongue to curse and speak evil. The Bible clearly states in Romans

12:14, "Bless them which persecute you: bless, and curse not."

My grandfather, who went to be with the Lord many years ago, had something dramatic happen in his life that changed my life. He was a devout Christian and a man that dedicated his later years to the Lord. My grandfather lived in a family house. One day, a personal item went missing in the house, and after a thorough search, they could not locate the missing item. My grandfather then suggested that a curse be placed on whoever stole the item. As he went to bed that night, the Lord visited him in his dream. In the dream, the Lord Jesus was telling my grandfather that he should have known better than suggesting that a curse be placed on someone. Jesus asked him, "Why would you curse with the same lips you worship me with?"

Immediately after that encounter in the dream with Jesus, my grandfather woke up blind. And for three days, someone who was agile and able to walk miles independently had to be held by the hand and led because he was blind. He immediately repented, and on the third night, the Lord Jesus appeared to him again in the dream and told him what to do to regain his sight—and as soon as he obeyed, my grandfather regained his sight instantly.

My grandfather's testimony of his encounter with Jesus regarding his use of the tongue has made me to be sensitive to the Spirit of God. I must watch it that the words that proceed out of my mouth and the meditation of my heart are acceptable in the sight of God (Psalm 19:14). What proceeds out of my mouth must be a blessing and not a curse; my tongue must be used in lifting people and not tearing them down, and my tongue must not be used to gossip or slander people. I must not be an agent of satan by using my tongue to bring division among brethren.

Not only are we not to curse, gossip, or slander other people, the Lord is saying we should bless others with our mouth regardless if they are our human friends or foe (Matthew 5:44). It may be that boy at school who is bullying you or the neighbor who is harassing you; the Lord is saying bless them and curse not. It could be a member in your own church who is always against you and does not love you; bless and love them. Pray that the Lord would change your heart and give you grace to love them. You always have to be heavenly conscious every minute of your waking hours. Do not be found wanting like the unwise virgins. Always be Rapture-ready. Keeping a grudge against someone is not worth your missing the Rapture or, worse yet, going to hell. May that not be our portion in Jesus name.

To emphasize the seriousness and the need for us to properly use our mouth, Jesus drew the multitudes together in Matthew 15:10-11 and said to them, "Hear and understand: Not that which goeth into the mouth defileth a man; but that which cometh out of the mouth, this defileth a man." Our body is the temple of God, a place where the Holy Spirit resides. We can easily defile it and make it inhabitable to the Holy Spirit by what we allow to proceed out of our mouth. Paul reminded us through his letter to the Corinthians saying, "Know ye not that ye are the temple of God, and that the Spirit of God dwelleth in you?" (1 Corinthians 3:16).

He then concluded in verse 17 by making it clear that if any man defiles the temple of God, God will destroy such a person.

May we not be candidates for God's destruction, in Jesus name. The Lord is calling us to a greater awareness in the use of our tongues because we shall eat of the fruit of our mouth. Proverbs 13:2 says, "A man shall eat good by the fruit of his mouth: but the soul of transgressors shall eat violence." May we not transgress against God by what proceeds out of our mouth, in Jesus name. God is calling us to rise to greater spiritual maturity with Him. He said "bless and curse not." Only uplifting words should come out of our mouth. We are to speak life and blessing, not curse and speak death. When we curse someone or speak death into their life, we are helping to fulfill the desire and agenda of satan, which is to steal, kill, and destroy people. It is never God's desire that the wicked perish (Ezekiel 33:11).

People ignorantly claim sickness and death upon themselves with what they say. Some will say they have a headache or that they have cancer. They are ignorantly claiming that disease for themselves. So as they claim the disease, it is established for them in the spiritual realm. The Bible clearly states in Matthew 18:18 that whatever we permit or declare on earth, that is what will be established in heaven. But if you say "I shall live and not die," then you are giving God the permission to work on your behalf. The reason most people don't make progress in life is because they speak blessing one moment and death and doubt the next minute. Until we determine in our hearts to consistently stand on the Word of God and speak only blessings, we will not begin to enjoy the fullness of God's provisions.

3. Not speaking the Word of Faith

Another reason some believers do not walk in dominion is because they walk by sight and not by faith. We are spiritual beings, and God created us in His spiritual image and likeness. It is the tendency of a natural man to make decisions based on the five senses of touch, sight, taste, smell, and hearing. But as believers, we forget that when we received Jesus as our Lord and Savior, the Holy Spirit took residence in us, and we became dead to the flesh and the desires of it. We are no longer led by the flesh rather by our spirit man through the guidance of the Holy Spirit.

Where we make our crucial error is not having faith in the Spirit of God to lead us; we are more comfortable placing our faith in our flesh and its five senses to guide us. So when God's Word says, "I am healed by the stripe of Jesus because he bore my sickness on the cross, then by faith, I must believe that and begin to operate according to my faith." In other words, confessing that I am healed and acting like am healed already even when I have not yet seen the physical manifestation of the healing, that is faith—believing and trusting in God's words and promises and backing it with your actions and spoken words even when you have not received the tangible evidence of what you hoped for. The Bible tells us that without this faith, it is impossible to please God. If God is not pleased with you, how can you be fruitful and live a life of dominion?

In Genesis 22, we read the story of Abraham when God commanded him to take his only son and offer him as a burnt offering to God. It is odd to know that Abraham, who waited over two decades for his promised son, Isaac, did not flinch or question God's authority over his son. The Bible recorded that Abraham rose up early in the morning, saddled his donkey, and took Isaac and two of his servants along to the place that God told him to sacrifice his son. On getting to the land of Moriah after three days of journey, Abraham located the place far ahead of him and spoke a statement of faith to his servant that tremendously turned Isaac's situation of death to one of life. The fact was clear—Isaac was to face death and be sacrificed to God. But instead of speaking death, Abraham spoke life to his situation. He told his servant in verse 5, "And Abraham said unto his young men, abide ye here with the ass; and I and the lad will go yonder and worship, and come again to you." Abraham said, "Isaac and I will be coming back after the sacrifice." Abraham has no way of knowing that his son, Isaac, will be coming back home with him, but he spoke life and told his servants, "Wait here, for Isaac and I are going up to worship God and the two of us will come back to you." God honored Abraham's word of faith, Isaac's life was spared, and the two of them came back exactly as he spoke.

Another instance when Abraham was not moved by sight but spoke words of faith was in verses 7 and 8 of Genesis 22 when Isaac asked his father, "Where is the wood and lamb for the burnt offering?" Abraham responded in verse 8, "And Abraham said, my son, God will provide himself a lamb for a burnt offering: so they went both of them together." Abraham could have said, "Isaac, you are the one to be sacrificed," but he did not speak death; rather he spoke the substance of things he hoped for. He said to Isaac,

"The Lord will provide the lamb." And what did God do? He honored Abraham's word of faith and provided the lamb for the burnt offering. Praise God! Hebrews 11:1 states, "Now faith is the substance of things hoped for, the evidence of things not seen."

Are you in a similar situation or are you facing a different challenge in life? Begin to speak life into your situation and watch God honor your word of faith.

Death and life are in the power of the tongue:
and they that love it shall eat the fruit thereof.
—Proverbs 18:21 (KJV)

4. Not standing on the Word of God

The Word of God is another powerful weapon you have at your disposal as a believer to live a victorious life of dominion. The Word of God, once spoken in faith, will never return void, but it will always accomplish that which it is sent to do.

When we begin to murmur instead of speaking the Word of God in our challenges, this can hinder our victorious walk in dominion. The Israelites prayed for years while in slavery in Egypt because they wanted a homeland of their own. The Lord answered their prayers and sent Moses to lead them out of Egypt into the land God promised them, which was flowing with milk and honey. But a majority of them did not lay eyes on the Promised Land because of their murmuring and disobedience. When we murmur, we are, in essence, saying we do not believe God can resolve this challenge facing us. If God cannot do it, who else can? May I not receive what God is not able to provide for me. The Bible warns us in Philippians 4:6, "Be careful for nothing; but in everything by prayer and supplication with thanksgiving let your request be made known unto God."

In other words, do not be anxious in anything in life. Rather, you should give thanks to God in prayer. In Job chapter 1, we read about a devout man of God named Job, who was perfect in the sight of the Lord because he loved the Lord to the extent that he feared doing anything evil that would displease God. Even when his seven sons and three daughters had a feast together and parties in their homes, Job would offer the best sacrifice to God for each of his children peradventure they sinned against God while they were celebrating.

It happened that as God was overly proud of Job, stating to satan how there is no one like Job on the earth, a perfect and upright man, satan incited God to remove his hedge of protection from Job and his family to see if Job will not curse God to His face. So God granted satan access to Job's family and his wealth. Immediately, satan went out of the presence of God to practice what he does best, which is to steal, kill, and destroy. As soon as Job heard the terrible news of the instant death of his seven sons and three daughters and the total loss of his possessions, he rose up, tore his robe, shaved his hair, fell to the ground, and worshiped God. He did not blame God or murmur against Him when his wife advised him to curse God and die. His reply to his wife was "You speak as one of the foolish women speaks. Shall we indeed accept good from God, and shall we not accept adversity?" (Job 2:10). The Bible then stated in Job 2:10b that "in all of this, Job did not sin with his lips."

When adversity comes your way, can God count on you not to sin with your lips? Make up your mind today to always give thanks to God no matter the circumstance.

It is easy to give thanks to God when everything is going good and you are on top, but what will you do when your faith is tested?

The way you use your tongue and exercise your faith will determine if you will enjoy a successful life or a defeated one. May the words that proceed out of your mouth be acceptable in the sight of God, in Jesus name. Amen.

Chapter 3

LIVING IN OBEDIENCE TO GOD

Obedience is the key to most breakthroughs in life. If we want to prosper in every aspect of our lives, we must be obedient to the Word of God. If we want to rule and have dominion, we must be obedient to God.

> *If they obey and serve him, they shall spend their days in prosperity, and their years in pleasures.*
>
> —Job 36:11

The Merriam-Webster Dictionary defines *obedience* as "an act or instance of obeying." So obedience is an act. It is doing what God asks you to do and how He wants you to do it and at the time He wants you to do it.

Until your obedience is prompt, it is not complete obedience. Obedience is not lip service. If I ask my son to mow the lawn, and for one reason or the other, he did not mow the lawn, then he has disobeyed. Likewise, when God commands us to love one another or live a holy life, and we fail to honor His words, then we have disobeyed and sinned.

The consequence of disobedience to God is spiritual death, and believe me, that is no life. The Bible warns us in Mark 8:36, saying, "For what shall it profit a man, if he shall gain the whole world and lose his own soul?" What kind of life are we living? Is it a life of obedience to God or a life architected by us and void of God? In the eyes of the world, it may seem that we are living the good life and succeeding without God. But God is compassionate and long-suffering, wishing that none should perish but rather that men should repent of their sin and accept His beloved Son, whom He freely sacrificed for the world for the redemption of sins. After it is all said and done, and you are standing before the Lord in judgment, what are you going to say? How would you explain to the King of kings? Are you going to say, "I did it my way"? Sorry to announce this, but that's not going to cut it. Jesus is a righteous judge, and He will judge us for the way we have lived our lives. For believers in Jesus Christ, the judgment seat of Christ is not a judgment unto condemnation; rather, it is a judgment to determine if we get a reward from the Lord.

For we must all appear before the judgment seat of Christ; that everyone may receive the things done in his body, according to that he hath done, whether it be good or bad.

—2 Corinthians 5:10

But the white-throne judgment is reserved solely for unbelievers, and it is for condemnation (Revelation 20:11-15). In Matthew 7:21-23, Jesus warns us that "not everyone that saith unto me, Lord, Lord, shall enter into the kingdom of heaven; but he that doeth the will of my Father which is in heaven. Many will say to me in that day, Lord, Lord, have we not prophesied in thy name? And in thy name have cast out devils? And in thy name done many wonderful works? And then will I profess unto them, I never knew you: depart from me, ye that work iniquity."

May we never be cast out from God's presence, in Jesus name. So Jesus is warning us that only those who do the will of His Father will enter the kingdom of heaven. So the question is, what is the will of God? It is the will of God that you hunger and thirst for righteousness (Matthew 5:6); it is the will of God that you love Him and love others (Luke 10:27); it is the will of God that you live a holy life (1 Peter 1:15-16). It is the will of God that you walk perfectly with Him (Matthew 5:48); it is the will of God that you depart from iniquity (2 Timothy 2:19), and it is the will of God that you obey Him (John 14:15), just to name a few.

Some people jokingly say that cats have nine lives. We all know it is not true, but one thing that is certain is that our days on this earth are numbered, and we only have this one life to get it right; because after death, there is judgment.

Hebrews 9:27 states, "And as it is appointed unto men once to die, but after this the judgment."

No amount of human effort that is void of Jesus Christ is good enough to take us to heaven. We need the saving grace of God, which requires us to receive by faith the sacrifice of Jesus on the cross for the atonement of our sins. Salvation is a free gift of God, and no man can work or pay for it because as it is stated in Isaiah 64:6, "But we are all as an unclean thing, and all our righteousness are as filthy rags; and we all do fade as a leaf; and our iniquities, like the wind, have taken us away." All our good works without Jesus Christ as our personal Savior is like a filthy rag. God does not value them, and He will not accept them as substitute for salvation. When we surrender totally to Jesus, the Spirit of God comes into us and gives us the grace to live a holy and obedient life. For the Bible tells us in Romans 3:23, "For all have sinned, and come short of the glory of God." No man can boast that he made it to heaven with his own goodwill.

> *As it is written, There is none righteous, no not one; There is none that understandeth, there is none that seeketh after God. They are all gone out of the way, they are together become unprofitable; there is none that doeth good, no, not one.*
>
> —Romans 3:10-12

This is why the Bible says *now* is the time of salvation, not tomorrow—now. If you are ready to secure your future today in Christ Jesus, say this short prayer with me now.

> *Father, I realized that I am a sinner, and I have sinned against you in my thoughts, my words, and in my actions. I ask you now to wash me clean with the blood of Jesus and forgive me my sins. Jesus, I accept you as my Lord and Savior, and I believe that you died for me on the cross and you rose again to be with the Father in heaven. As from today, I give my life to you. Write my name in the book of life. Thank you, Father, for saving me, and in Jesus name, I pray. Amen.*

If you sincerely said that prayer, you are now a child of God. Congratulations! Tell someone about your newfound faith in Jesus. Also, I want you to find a Bible-believing church and attend church regularly to strengthen your faith. Get the Holy Bible and start reading the Word of your Heavenly Father.

BENEFITS OF OBEDIENCE TO GOD

1. LONG LIFE

A benefit of obedience to God is long life. Jesus gave us a new commandment in Matthew 22:37, which states, "Thou shall love the Lord thy God with all thy heart and with all thy soul and with all thy mind." One of the benefits of obeying this commandment to love God is divine protection and long life (Psalm 91:14-16). On the other hand, when we disobey God, we fall in danger of cutting our lives short.

As I Studied the generations of the offspring of Adam in Genesis 5, I discovered that most of Adam's offspring's from Adam to Lamech lived an average of over nine hundred years. But in Genesis chapter 6, God saw that the wickedness of men was very rampant and increasing, so God cut short the life span of man from the average age of over 900 years to 120 (Genesis 6:3). He stated that His Spirit will no longer strive with man, and man's number of days was cut short. It was the wickedness of men that caused man's life span to be drastically reduced.

On the other hand, obedience to God can cause God to prolong your life. Take the case of King Hezekiah in Isaiah 38:1-7. So it was that King Hezekiah was sick unto death, and Prophet Isaiah came to him to warn the king to get his house in order because his appointed time on earth was up, for the Lord was about to take him. Instead of accepting his fate, King Hezekiah turned his head toward the wall and prayed fervently, asking the Lord to remember how he has walked before the Lord in truth and with a perfect heart and has obeyed and done what is good in the sight of God. Just as Prophet Isaiah was heading home after delivering the message to the king, God intercepted him and told him to return to King Hezekiah with a new message. "This time to tell the king that he shall live and not die, that the God of David had added fifteen more years to his life." This was, of course, good news to King Hezekiah. May your obedience to God and perfect walk with Him cause your life to be to prolonged in Jesus name.

2. BLESSING

If ye walk in my statutes, and keep my commandments, and do them; then I will give you rain in due season and the land shall yield her increase, and the trees of the field shall yield their fruit.

—Leviticus 26:3-4

Without rain or water, no land can be fertile to sustain life, and no tree can yield its fruit. Same way without God's blessing and intervention in your career, business, or ministry, no man can survive. It is the finger of God that causes you to prosper. Except the Lord builds your career, business, ministry, or marital life, any attempt by anyone to build without God is building in vain (Psalm 127:1). When you obey the Lord, all His blessings will come upon you (Deuteronomy 28:2-8). When we obey God, we enter into His divine and supernatural provision (Genesis 22:15-18).

The scripture above (Leviticus 26:3-4) gives us an open access into the limitless reserve of God's blessings. With every promise, there is a condition attached to it—a condition that we have to fulfill. God always keeps His end of the bargain; humanity, on the other hand, might not keep their promise. But we serve a God that will not fail us or back off from His promise. When we seek first the kingdom of God and His righteousness then all these blessings of God that people are yearning to receive will be ours (Matthew 6:33). God's blessing is part of our inheritance. There are things in the kingdom of God that do not need us to fast and pray for. All we need to do is walk in complete obedience to God, and these things will be ours with ease.

The Bible tells us that there was once a famine in the land of Gerar where Isaac dwelled, and the natural thing for Isaac to do was to move to Egypt, but the Lord gave him a clear instruction not to leave for Egypt (Genesis 26:1-6, 12-14). To the natural man, this instruction from God does not make any sense; moving to Egypt where there is abundance would seem to be the sensible choice. So Isaac obeyed God and planted crop in the land of Gerar, and that same year, he reaped hundredfold harvests—and not only that, Isaac became so wealthy that King Abimelek and the Philistines became envious of him. Then King Abimelek asked Isaac to move away because he had become so powerful for them (Genesis 26:12-16).

When we obey God, He will turn a desert land into a fertile ground for us. As we obey God, He will cause His blessings to overshadow us. Our way is certainly not God's way, and His thought is not our thought (Isaiah 55:8). God kept Isaac from Egypt because He knew that at a point in the history of Israel, Egypt will represent bondage, a departure from the perfect plan of God for His people. Obedience will keep you from everything that represents bondage. It will allow you to eat or get your blessings in due season. This means as we obey God, we will enjoy all our redemptive blessings in due season. There shall be no delay in your blessing in Jesus mighty name. Obedience is the vehicle that transports us into God's supernatural provision and lifestyle. May God grant you the grace to live in obedience to Him in Jesus name.

WE MUST BE DOERS OF GOD'S WORD

It pays to obey God, and it also costs much when you decide to disobey God. The choice is ours. God has set before us life and death, and he wants us to choose life. He will never force us against our will. It is our choice to make.

> *See, I have set before thee this day life and good, and death and evil; In that I command thee this day to love the Lord thy God, to walk in His ways, and to keep His commandments and his statutes and his judgments, that thou mayest live and multiply: and the Lord God shall bless thee in the land whither thou goest to possess it.*
>
> —Deuteronomy 30:15-16

Abraham was blessed when he obeyed God and did not withhold his only son from God. The Bible said Abraham rose early in the morning. He did not wait to think about it or seek human opinion. Rather, he rose early in the morning to carry out God's request. How is your walk with God? When God speaks to your heart, do you obey immediately or do you seek signs or a second opinion? God is looking for those who will obey his command without delay. Because of his obedience, Abraham was blessed and multiplied in that he was blessed with numerous flocks and herds, silver and gold, male and female servants, camels and donkeys (Genesis 22:16-17).

> *Therefore whosoever heareth these sayings of mine and doeth them, I will liken him unto a wise man which built his house upon a rock: And the rain descended, and the floods came and the winds blew and beat upon that house; and it fell not: for it was founded upon a rock.*
>
> —Matthew 7:24-25

> *Wherefore it shall come to pass, if ye hearken to these judgments, and keep, and do them, that the Lord thy God shall keep unto thee the covenant and the mercy which he sware unto thy fathers*
>
> —Deuteronomy 7:12

> *Keep therefore the words of this covenant, and do them, that ye may prosper in all that ye do.*
>
> —Deuteronomy 29:9

One way we honor God is to live a life of obedience. It means deciding in your heart today, with the help of the Holy Spirit, that you will live a life of obedience to God.

And why call ye me, Lord, Lord, and do not the things which I say?

—Luke 6:46

Some may say, "I am still young. Let me enjoy the pleasure of sin now and repent later when I am old." That is playing Russian roulette with your life. God cannot be mocked, for whatever a man sows, so shall he reap (Galatians 6:7). Now is the accepted time of salvation, and your tomorrow is not promised. The Bible states in James 4:14, "For what is your life? It is even a vapour, that appeareth for a little time, and then vanisheth." If you read further in verses 16 to 17 of the NASB, it states, "But as it is, you boast in your arrogance; all such boasting is evil. Therefore, to one who knows the right thing to do and does not do it, to him it is sin." So when God says do not fornicate, and we go ahead and do it, then it is sin, and we must repent and do it no more.

Disobedience was the reason why Adam and Eve fell from grace. May you and I never fall from grace, in Jesus name. Amen. They had it made—a life of luxury and abundance. All they had to do was tend the garden God gave to them and rule over God's creation. Adam and Eve did not have to worry about where the next meal was coming from or how they would pay the next bill. God supplied all their needs. Because of their disobedience, their life was transformed from one of living in a penthouse to one of living in a poorhouse. Adam now had to work for every food he placed on his family's table. Thank God for sending Jesus to pay for our sins for whosoever believes in him shall not perish (John 3:16).

So I ask you, how do you feel when your son or daughter disobeys you right in your face? Now how do you think God feels? "Come now, and let us reason together, saith the Lord: though your sins be as scarlet, they shall be as white as snow; though they be red like crimson, they shall be as wool" (Isaiah 1:18).

Is this not a great and generous offer from our Creator that loves us? The price has been paid for your sin, all you need now is to repent from your sin and accept this free offer of grace. Are you going to listen to him and walk his way or will you harden your heart and do it your way? Remember, you have been bought with a precious price, and that price is the blood of Jesus that He shed on the cross for you and me. We no longer answer to the evil one but to God Almighty. Momentary pleasure of sin is not worth going to hell and being separated eternally from the God that loves you.

Disobedience not only brings spiritual death but a curse to the unrepentant heart.

In Genesis 3:16-17, the Lord made it clear to Adam and Eve that if they did not heed His Word on that day, they will surely die. The same day Adam and Eve sinned against the Lord, that same day, they lost their relationship with God and that was spiritual death. The Lord stopped visiting them as He regularly did prior to their sinful act; the Lord shut them out of the garden. Thank God that He made a way for you and me to enjoy his presence again. You see, God loves us so much that He made plans for you and me to eventually unite with him through the death of Jesus. It is not the will of God that any should perish but rather that all will come to repentance and receive the free grace of God. The Holy Spirit is the one that draws men to God; if He is leading you today, don't harden your heart.

Our time here on earth is short compared to eternity, so do the wise thing and start planning on how you will spend eternity after your present life on earth ends. It is simple. God has done it all for mankind. It is so simple that many have missed the mark.

WE ARE THE LIGHT OF THE WORLD

Most of us believers are serving God with lip service while our actions are totally different from what we profess, and it makes people wonder if we are true disciples of

Christ. Satan is not worried or concerned that you go to church, sing in the choir, or perform all the religious activities. But one thing satan would go out of his way to stop you from doing is living that life you profess as a Christian.

Honoring God is more than lip service; it has to do with the way we conduct ourselves. Do people see Jesus in the way you live? Do they see the light of God in you? Do people want to know more about Jesus because of the way you conduct yourself?

> *Let your light so shine before men, that they may see your good works and glorify your Father which is in Heaven.*
>
> —Matthew 5:16 (NKJV)

The Word of God is saying to us that we should allow the light of God in us to shine brightly so that men will give Him glory. The truth is that if you are placed in a dark, crowded room, it would be difficult to navigate your way without bumping into someone or something. But once a light is introduced into that same room, you will find it a lot easier to navigate your way. That source of light provided a light on your path. Likewise, as Christians and followers of Christ, we are the light of the world. There has to be a difference between believers in Jesus Christ and nonbelievers. In this end-time, it is very difficult to tell a Christian from a non-Christian. We have adopted the ways of the world. We are eating and drinking and giving ourselves to lustful desires, pursuing the world's wealth while souls are trooping to hell per second. We have copied the world's style of dressing. It is not uncommon to go to most churches on Sundays or weekdays and find Christians with tight-fitting and body-hugging clothes practically revealing their sensual body parts all in the name of the latest fashion; and instead of repenting, we are consoling ourselves that God only looks at the heart. As a man thinketh in his heart so he is (Proverbs 23:7). The evidence of our living a chaste life reflects not only from the inside but also outwardly.

The question is, if Jesus was physically present in our weekly service, how will we dress? But the fact is, Jesus is always present. Because we do not see Him with our physical eyes does not mean He is absent. We should not allow our actions or mode of dressing to cause others to sin. The Bible says in 1 Corinthians 8:13, "Wherefore, if meat make my brother to offend, I will eat no flesh while the world standeth, least I make my brother to offend." In other words, if my action causes others to sin, then I need to refrain from that action. If my provocative way of dressing is causing others to lust and sin, then I must change the way I dress so God will be glorified.

Let your holy life prompt others to live holy, and let your unpolluted conversation prompt others to speak chastely. Let your life of obedience prompt others to want to emulate you, and let your good deed prompt others to do likewise. Let your love for friends and human foes distinguish you as a child of God and make others experience the love of God.

Some have stood on the scripture verse in Exodus 22:18, which states, "Thou shall not suffer a witch to live." They have turned this verse as an open invitation to war against their human enemies. We have excitedly and joyfully called on the Holy Spirit to become our private assassin. We have prayed and called on the death of Islamic militants and those who hate us.

We must not be quick to forget that we war not against flesh and blood but against demonic spirits, principalities and powers, rulers of darkness and spiritual wickedness in high places (Ephesians 6:12). Our war was never meant to be against our fellow flesh-and-blood brothers and sisters but against the spiritual power that is controlling that person. That demonic spirit working behind the scene is our real enemy.

It is never the desire of God that wicked men should perish and go to hell but that they come to repentance

(2 Peter 3:9). So why do we pray that they should perish? Our God never takes pleasure in the death of the wicked, so why are we so excited and taking pleasure in calling for the death of another person? Jesus did not lay a curse on those that crucified Him. He did not even call for their deaths. He simply forgave them.

> *Beloved if God so loved us, we ought also to love one another.*
> —1 John 4:11

Loving does not mean only those in our circle of friends. If we practice such love, what reward do we expect from God? Even unbelievers do the same (Luke 6:32). The love of God knows no bounds and so must our love. Enough of our selective love. The hour has come for us to change our ways. Jesus said in Matthew 5:43-44, "Ye have heard that it hath been said, thou shalt love thy neighbor, and hate thine enemy. But I say unto you, Love your enemies, bless them that curse you, do good to them that hate you, and pray for them which despitefully use you, and persecute you."

In other words, we should wish no one any harm. Love those that are unlovable, and pray that God will change your heart so you can be an instrument of God's light in this very dark world.

Apostle Paul was like a modern-day terrorist. He targeted Christians, and he made sure he witnessed their deaths to the extent that some of the disciples of Christ went into hiding. If he was in this era, many would have prayed for his death. But God turned this terrorist of a man into one of the greatest apostles the church has ever known and channeled his zeal for the kingdom's use. Paul later wrote almost half of the New Testament as he was inspired by the Holy Spirit. God does not take pleasure in writing people off; we should not attempt to do so.

So if we hate those terrorists and those that try to kill us, we are not loving; rather, we have become like them, murderers and terrorists in the eyes of God.

The Word of God says in 1 John 3:15, "Whosoever hateth his brother is a murderer: and ye know that no murderer hath eternal life abiding in him."

We are made in the image of God, so let us reflect Him. In the midst of your friends and coworkers, reflect Him; in the midst of your family, reflect Him; and as a missionary in a strange land, reflect Him. We must allow the Holy Spirit to teach and prune us so we can be more like Jesus daily. To conceal or hide our light is to betray the trust Jesus has in us. May we not betray Him in Jesus name.

In Matthew 25:30, the unprofitable servant was cast into the outer darkness. We are called to preach the Gospel to those in the dark world. Most of us Christians are uncomfortable sharing their faith with others. Not sharing your faith is like being on a boat and watching others drown and not doing anything to help them. May our lives bring honor and profit to the kingdom of God in Jesus name.

Chapter 4

FORGIVENESS

WHAT IS FORGIVENESS?

I will define forgiveness as letting go of any offense someone has instigated against you and relinquishing your right to retaliate against that person.

Without the Lord forgiving us our sins, we would have been doomed to spend eternity in hell separated from the Lord. Are you not excited and glad to know that God forgave your sins? I know I am. It is so exciting to know of this good news that you want to shout it at the rooftop and to your neighbors, friends, and loved ones. The good news that I have been forgiven by Jesus is too much for me to bear alone. I see every soul so precious in the eyes of the Lord, and I know the Lord is counting on me to tell them about Him. It is not uncommon for me to share the good news to total strangers as the Lord leads me because the love of God drives me to do so. And I pray that the zeal of God will come upon you in Jesus mighty name.

So the Lord forgiving our sin is key to our entering the kingdom of God, and this was accomplished by the shedding of blood. The shedding of blood was necessary for the atonement of our sins. When the blood of animals was not sufficient to cleanse us from our sins, God sent Jesus, His only begotten Son, to come on earth in the form of a man for the atonement of our sins so that whosoever believes in Him would not perish but receive eternal life (John 3:16).

Contrary to popular belief, our salvation is not based on how good we are personally or how much we have contributed to humanity. You will be surprised how many people truly believe that if they have a good heart and do the right thing, they will make heaven when they die. I heard of a popular TV host making such a claim. The fact is that the Bible declares in Romans 3:23, "For all have sinned and come short of the glory of God; being justified freely by his grace through the redemption that is in Christ Jesus." So except we come to the one that has the key to the kingdom of God, how can we expect to enter? If, for example, a wealthy individual is having a dinner party for his family and friends, and someone else attempted to join others to get in, that person cannot be granted access because that person does not have a relationship with the host, and the person's name is not on the guest list. And if they attempted to come in by force, then they will be arrested and thrown in jail. In the same way, Jesus considers someone that is trying to enter heaven without Him a thief. Jesus has already told us that

> *I am the way, the truth, and the life: no man cometh unto the Father, but by me.*
>
> —John 14:6

There is no other way for your sins to be forgiven; it is only through Jesus Christ. Ephesians 1:7 states, "In whom we have redemption through his blood, the forgiveness of sins, according to the riches of his grace." And the Lord added in Hebrews 10:17, "And their sins and iniquities will I remember no more." I do not know about you, but I just want to jump for joy anytime I hear these words. God said He will remember my sin no more! Wow, that is something to celebrate.

Our salvation is not based on our membership or affiliation to a church or how much time we attended church programs; rather, our salvation is the free grace of God as we are reminded in Ephesians 2:8, "For by grace are ye saved through faith; and that not of yourselves: it is the gift of God: Not of works, lest any man should boast."

LOVE AND FORGIVENESS

Matthew West, a popular Christian artist, wrote a song called "Forgiveness" based on a letter written to him by a young lady that lost one of her twin daughters to a drunk driver as she was traveling home with her friend. The young man who killed her daughter was sentenced to a long prison term, and the woman spent her days doing public speaking about the dangers of drunk driving. In one of these events, Jesus spoke to her heart that she had not forgiven the young man who killed her daughter. So she went to the prison and told the young man that she forgave him. The young man who killed her daughter was moved by her gesture that he stated, "I could not forgive myself yet she forgave me?" and added that he found internal salvation through that forgiveness. The story did not end there. The young woman who lost her daughter went further to petition the court to reduce the young man's sentence, which was granted. When asked why she did that, she simply stated, "So that he will have a second chance." What a story of love and forgiveness.

The kingdom of God operates on love and forgiveness, and we cannot truthfully say we belong to this kingdom if we are not living a life of love and forgiveness.

We must learn to forgive others if we expect God to forgive us our sins. It is impossible to say that someone will not offend you; even Jesus was offended when they turned

His house of prayer into a den of thieves. But what we have control of is the power to forgive. I personally operate in advance forgiveness, the concept of forgiving others before they even commit the offence. That means I have already proposed in my heart that no matter what the circumstance or what the offence is, I will forgive. It is a concept I believe God will give you the grace to embrace.

How Do We Forgive Others?

1. By annulment of their trespasses

Jesus made it clear in Matthew 6:14, "For if ye forgive men their trespasses, your heavenly Father will also forgive you."

We must begin to see sin as a debt that must be paid. Our sin was paid by the blood of Jesus, but what if someone offends you? Then that becomes a debt that is owed to you. The decision you take from that moment will determine where you spend eternity as a believer. If you choose not to forgive, then the Lord has no obligation to also forgive you. So for our forgiveness to be complete, we must totally annul that person's trespass against us.

2. By asking God to heal our wounded hearts

When someone offends you or someone you love breaks the trust that existed between both of you, it hurts; and until the Lord heals your heart, you may feel pain whenever that person's name is mentioned. The healing starts when you verbally release that person from your heart. You call that person's name and say "I forgive you, and I pray that God bless you." If you do not forgive and release them, then your joy cannot be full because that person still controls the fullness of your joy. The sooner you ask God to heal your heart and release that person, the better you will begin to feel. As you release and forgive the person, all your stress and anxiety begin to go away.

3. BY RELINQUISHING OUR RIGHT TO RETALIATE

When we forgive, we must also relinquish our rights to repay that person for what they did to us. The Bible tells us that vengeance does not belong to us, it is of the Lord (Romans 12:19). It is not my job to repay, so I must relinquish that right and take that option off my table. I must take myself out of the picture of retribution and allow God to take His rightful place. Our God is a just God and a righteous judge, and I am likely to mess things up if I want to avenge myself.

4. BY PRAYING FOR THAT PERSON

The quickest way to have your wounded heart healed is to pray for that person that offended you. As you do so, your hatred for that person is lifted, the love of God takes its rightful place in your heart, and victory from the spirit of unforgiveness is delivered to you. In Luke 6, the Lord taught us how we are to forgive those that offended us.

> *But I say unto you which hear, Love your enemies, do good to them which hate you, bless them that curse you, and pray for them which despitefully use you.*
>
> —Luke 6:27-28

You Owe It to Him to Forgive Others

As Christ has forgiven us, we owe it to Him to forgive others who have trespassed against us.

> *Then came Peter to him, and said, Lord, how oft shall my brother sin against me, and I forgive him? till seven times? Jesus saith unto him, I say not unto thee, Until seven times: but, Until seventy times seven.*
>
> *Therefore is the kingdom of heaven likened unto a certain king, which would take account of his servants.*

And when he had begun to reckon, one was brought unto him, which owed him ten thousand talents.

But forasmuch as he had not to pay, his lord commanded him to be sold, and his wife, and children, and all that he had, and payment to be made.

The servant therefore fell down, and worshipped him, saying, Lord, have patience with me, and I will pay thee all.

Then the lord of that servant was moved with compassion, and loosed him, and forgave him the debt.

But the same servant went out, and found one of his fellow servants, which owed him an hundred pence: and he laid hands on him, and took him by the throat, saying, Pay me that thou owest.

And his fellow servant fell down at his feet, and besought him, saying, Have patience with me, and I will pay thee all.

And he would not: but went and cast him into prison, till he should pay the debt.

So when his fellow servants saw what was done, they were very sorry, and came and told unto their lord all that was done.

Then his lord, after that he had called him, said unto him, O thou wicked servant, I forgave thee all that debt, because thou desiredst me:

Shouldest not thou also have had compassion on thy fellow servant, even as I had pity on thee?

And his lord was wroth, and delivered him to the tormentors, till he should pay all that was due unto him.

So likewise shall my heavenly Father do also unto you, if ye from your hearts forgive not everyone his brother their trespasses.

—Matthew 18:21-35

The parable Jesus gave was of a servant that owed ten thousand talents to his master. When the servant could not pay his debt, he pleaded for mercy, and his master took pity on him and forgave him. Meanwhile, as the servant stepped out, he saw a fellow servant that owed him money. He immediately demanded his money, but his fellow servant was not able to pay and begged for mercy instead. This servant refused; instead, he grabbed his fellow servant by the throat and demanded his money. When his master heard of what he did to his fellow servant, he demanded to know why the servant did not forgive knowing that his own debts were forgiven. Then the master became furious with him and delivered him to be tormented.

This is not just a story but a parable that represents how the kingdom of God operates. The master represents the Lord who died on the cross for us for the forgiveness of our sins, and the servant represents you and me. As a servant of God, we have received mercy and forgiveness from the Lord, and we owe it to the Lord to forgive all others that have trespassed against us. We have to be very conscious to live in peace with all men because if you fail to forgive your fellow man in your heart, God cannot forgive you your sins, and it could mean eternity separated from the Lord. Today is the day to release everyone that has offended you. Set them free in your heart, forgive them, and live a life of peace with all men. I pray that the Lord give you the grace today to forgive in advance even before someone offends you.

Chapter 5

MESSAGE FOR GOD'S SERVANTS

A servant is anyone serving God in any capacity as His ambassador. I applaud you for your faithful service. May the Lord grant you exceeding grace to finish your race strong in Jesus name. As the coming of the Lord draws near, it is even more urgent that we intensify our service for the Lord. Jesus declares in John 9:4 that "I must work the works of him that sent me, while it is day: the night cometh, when no man can work." It is important that every faithful believer continues to remain focused on his or her spiritual race and not get distracted. Below are God's words that will help us triumph to the end.

BE FRUITFUL AND SERVE GOD FAITHFULLY

The Lord has chosen and ordained you to serve the body of Christ and to bring forth fruit that will abide. The Bible says, "Ye have not chosen me, but I have chosen you, and ordained you, that ye should go and bring forth fruit, and that your fruit should remain: that whatsoever ye shall ask of the Father in my name, he may give it you" (John 15:16).

The call of God in the life of any man or woman is an unmerited privilege, and to be chosen and set apart for the master's use is the greatest honor. So as a servant of God and His ambassador, we are privileged to be called and honored to be chosen. Being called and chosen by God to be His ambassador is not something we should take lightly.

Matthew 22:14 states, "For many are called, but few are chosen." And God said in Jeremiah 1:5, "Before you were formed in your mother's womb I knew you, and before you were born, I set you apart as a prophet to the nations."

We must be faithful and fruitful at our appointed office. It does not matter if you are the greeter in the house of God or the Arch bishop, you are very valuable to God and must diligently carry out your assigned position so that when the master returns, He will find you faithful at your post. We serve not for man's reward or applause but for the love of Him that called us into His vineyard. Serve God with all your power and might. Let His zeal consume you. Jesus was consumed with the zeal to do His Father's business. He did not stand by and allow the house of God to be used as a marketplace by money changers. He took the mission His Father gave Him very personally. It was written concerning Jesus in John 2:17, "The zeal of thine house hath eaten me up."

God calls the unqualified and qualifies them and gives grace for the ones called to serve. It could be as a missionary to the unreached tribes of the world or service group in your local church. He will not leave you an orphan but will equip you with grace as you faithfully serve as co-laborer with Christ. In Psalm 84:10, King David made a profound statement that reveals our privileged position as a servant of the Most High God. He said, "I had rather be a doorkeeper in the house of my God, than to dwell in the tents of the wickedness." This is a king speaking and making a bold declaration that he would rather be a doorkeeper in the house of God than any other position the wicked world would give him. What a privilege and honor it is for us to be called to serve in the kingdom of our great God.

Paul was consumed with the zeal to preach the Gospel; not even a shipwreck, snake bite or jail could stop him. He declared in 1 Corinthians 9:16, "Woe is unto me, if I preach not the gospel." This is a man clearly on fire for God and was consumed with the zeal to finish the race strong and complete the task assigned to him by Jesus.

So in Ephesians 4:1, Paul pleaded with the ordained servants of God stating, "I therefore, the prisoner of the Lord, beseech you that ye walk worthy of the vocation wherewith ye are called."

Paul is beseeching us to make sure that we are about our Father's business. In verse 2 of the same chapter, Paul encouraged us to bear with one another with all humility, meekness, and lowliness of heart and to be patient and gentle with one another.

He went on to warn us in Ephesians 4:3 to guard against division in the body of Christ no matter what form it manifested. satan wants nothing more than to steal, kill, and destroy the body of Christ. So we must be vigilant in prayer and sober-minded in spirit so we can discern the wiles of the evil one.

Be committed to the service God has called you, and as you faithfully serve in the little, he will reward you with much responsibility by making you ruler of many (Matthew 25:14-30).

REACH OUT TO THE LOST SHEEP

The act of evangelism is dying in many churches. We have gotten so comfortable in our lives as Christians, that we no longer feel a sense of responsibility for a lost soul.

Lost souls are the heartbeat of God. If our purpose in life is not geared toward adding more souls to the kingdom of God, then we have not lived a fruitful life. In the parable of the lost sheep in Luke 15, Jesus spoke about a shepherd that had a hundred sheep. He left the ninety-nine to seek out the one that was lost and did not return until he found the lost sheep. The shepherd left the ninety-nine knowing that they were well fed and protected. He left to seek the one that was lost.

The Bible tells us in Luke 15:7, "I say unto you, that likewise joy shall be in heaven over one sinner that repenteth, more than over ninety and nine just persons, which need no repentance."

There is more joy in heaven over a lost soul that repented and came to the Lord than over the ones that are already saved. This tells me how important lost sheep are to my Heavenly Father. It tells me that our priority of putting more energy and focus on the saved instead of the lost is misguided. If half our congregation in our churches goes out for evangelism on regular bases to tell others about Jesus, we might be able, through the grace of God, to depopulate hell and decrease the numbers of people going into it daily.

The Bible reminds us in Proverbs 11:30, "The fruit of the righteous is a tree of life; and he that winneth souls is wise."

Let us get excited in seeking after the lost sheep. Receive the grace now in Jesus name.

BE A HUMBLE SERVANT

Jesus was very critical of the Pharisees because of their pretense to be holy. They pretended to love God but could not lift a finger to help those that are in need. They preferred rather to be served instead of serving others. We can also pretend to be humble, but the fact is, we cannot deceive God.

In 1 Peter 5:5, we are warned to clothe ourselves with humility because God resists the proud and renders grace to the humble. As servants of God, we must guide against thinking more highly of ourselves than we ought to especially when we begin to experience success in the ministry. We should not allow the enemy to feed us with ideas that our ministry's success was due to our own effort. Even when God elevates you and make you His kingdom star, you must remain humble and cultivate a heart of a servant. Philippians 2:5-7 exemplifies how Jesus being God made himself of no reputation and took the form of a servant. "Let this mind be in you, which was also in Christ Jesus: Who, being in the form of God, thought it not robbery to be equal with God: But made himself of no reputation, and took upon him the form of a servant, and was made in the likeness of men." This is the example Jesus set for us and we must emulate Him.

Just as we noticed in the life of King Saul, pride can cause well-meaning men and women of God to lose focus and be carried away as the world approves them. They run the danger of watering down the gospel and tailoring God's message to fit the mode of political correctness. This is the scheme of the enemy to steal, kill and destroy God's servants. So we must constantly be watchful and intercede in prayer for every servant of God.

Men can approve you and make you look great in the eyes of the world, but to be truly great, we must remain humble and be like the little children Jesus referred to in Matthew chapter 18. It is time to repent and get back to our Father's business of serving His people and reaching out for the lost.

> *At the same time came the disciples unto Jesus, saying, Who is the greatest in the kingdom of heaven? And Jesus called a little child unto him, and set him in the midst of them, And said, Verily I say unto you, Except ye be converted, and become as little children, ye shall not enter into the kingdom of heaven. Whosoever therefore shall humble himself as this little child, the same is greatest in the kingdom of heaven.*
>
> —Matthew 18:1-4

One of the characteristics of a child is humility. A servant of God that is prideful is not ready for service. We must be ready to roll up our sleeves when necessary and tend to a wounded sheep. God has called us to put on a heart of compassion and love toward his people. Colossians 3:12 explains it best, "Put on therefore, as the elect of God, holy and beloved, bowels of mercies, kindness, humbleness of mind, meekness, and longsuffering."

In 2 Corinthians 12:6-10, Apostle Paul stated that if he were to boast, he will be telling the truth. But choose not to boast because many will think of him more highly than necessary. As ministers of God, may we never boast of our strength, wealth, or achievements, but rather, may we acknowledge God for all our success. Let all boasting be unto the Lord for we are just a privileged vessel of God.

FEAR GOD

As servants of God, we need to have the fear of God as we serve Him. It is the fear of God that will deliver us from evil and keep us from compromising. Proverbs 3:7 says "Be not wise in thine own eyes: fear the Lord, and depart from evil." Joseph could not sin against God with Potiphar's wife because he feared the Lord. Job was a perfect man in the eyes of God because he feared the Lord and shunned evil (Job 1:8). Until we decide in our hearts to have a reverential fear of God, we will continue to be in contempt of His words. Romans 3:18 says about the wicked, "There is no fear of God before their eyes."

Our Heavenly Father is holy and righteous, and those who must walk with Him must be holy and righteous. And it starts with the fear of God. Let us therefore begin to delight in the Word of God and have respect for His ways (Psalm 119:15). See how Solomon, the wisest man in his time, concluded the matter of life. He stated,

> *Let us hear the conclusion of the whole matter:*
> *Fear God, and keep his commandments: for this is*
> *the whole duty of man.*
>
> —Ecclesiastes 12:13

FINAL WORD

Paul said, "I press toward the mark for the prize of the high calling of God in Christ Jesus" (Philippians 3:14).

Let us together remain faithful to our high calling and finish our race strong so that we may also join Paul in saying, "I have fought a good fight, I have finished my course, I have kept the faith; Henceforth there is laid up for me a crown of righteousness, which the Lord, the righteous judge, shall give me at that day and not to me only, but unto all them also that love his appearing" (2 Timothy 4:7-8).

Remain steadfast in your calling; let him that is diligent and just remain so, let him that is faithful remain faithful, let him that is holy and righteous remain holy and righteous still. Jesus is coming quickly to reward us for our works just as He stated beautifully in Revelation 22:12, "And, behold, I come quickly; and my reward is with me, to give every man according as his work shall be."

May the grace of God be with you, and may His exceeding grace sustain you. You shall not fail God in your service to Him. Your walk with God shall be blameless in the mighty name of Jesus. May the Lord find us as worthy servants, and at the end of our service here on earth, may He welcome us home with this saying, "Welcome home, good and faithful servant." I love you and God bless you!

Chapter 6

HOLINESS

WHAT IS HOLINESS?

The word *holy* is often misinterpreted by Christians to mean different things. Read the research conducted by Barna group.

When pressed to describe what it means to be holy, adults gave a wide range of answers. The most common reply was "I don't know," offered by one out of every five adults (21%). Other responses fell into categories such as "being Christ-like" (19%), making faith your top priority in life (18%), living a pure life or sinless lifestyles (12%), and having a good attitude about people and life (10%), Other response categories included focusing completely on God (9%), being guided by Holy Spirit (9%), being born again (8%), reflecting the character of

God (7%), Exhibiting a moral lifestyle (5%), and accepting and practicing biblical truth (5%). (*www. barna.org*)

With this variation of definition regarding holiness, it is apparent that we need to have a better understanding of holiness if we are to be as holy as we are called to be.

In Leviticus 11:44, the Lord commanded us to be holy as He is holy. The question is, what is holiness? From the *Wikipedia* Judaism definition, we discover the Hebrew noun for holiness is *kedushah* from the adjective *Kodesh*; "holy" meaning "separateness or set apart."

Why will a holy God call us to be holy knowing our limitation and weakness to sin as humans? One thing we can be assured of is that God will not require from us what he has not already equipped us or empowered us to do. That would be unfair to us.

Isaiah 40:25 describes God as the Holy One, which means He is set apart and unique—there is none like Him. In other words, there is no one that can be likened to Him or equal to Him. If there is no one that can be likened to God, why is He calling me to be holy like Him? The answer lies in the definition of holiness. In the years Jesus lived on the earth, He was holy, and He modeled what it meant to be holy. He stated in John 14:30 that satan has nothing on him because He never sinned nor allowed the world to influence Him. He set Himself apart from the worldly influences to do His Father's business. This is the model of holiness we must exhibit as followers of Christ. We must actively go about our Father's business and set ourselves apart from the world, not allow the world to influence us culturally, spiritually, or morally. This is the essence of our call to be holy just as our Lord is holy.

WHO DID GOD CALL TO BE HOLY?

God has called the church to be holy, and that means you and me. We are a chosen generation, a royal priesthood before God. We are a holy people of God set apart for the Master's use, and we are special and peculiar people of God who are called out of darkness into His wonderful light.

> *But ye are a chosen generation, a royal priesthood, and holy nation, a peculiar people; that should shew forth the praises of him who hath called you out of darkness into His marvelous light.*
> —1 Peter 2:9 (KJV)

The Lord has called every born-again believer out of darkness to a life that is dedicated to Him and separated from worldly influences. We are set apart from the world for the Master's use; the Bible says although we live in this world, we are not part of it (John 15:19). Be very wary when the world begins to love and approve you; is it because you stand with them and you are now one of them? There was an uproar in the gay community in the United States when an owner of a popular fast-food chain, who is a Christian, stated publicly that he does not support and believe in gay marriage. There was a backlash from the gay community and other sectors of the public. Many were calling for a boycott of his chains of restaurants, and some wanted the restaurant out of their states. This is the world we live in; when you stand for Jesus and His righteousness, they will hate you because you are not one of them.

We cannot say we are Christians and continue to indulge in the various sins the world packages for us. There must be a visible difference between a Christian and a non-Christian. In our conversation with others, there must be a difference. We cannot be like the world and talk like the world. We must guide against what we allow our eyes to see and our ears to hear. The enemy of our souls is working night and day to influence us with filthy things of this world through the devices we already have in our home such as the television and computer. He wants to take advantage of us, but we should not be ignorant of his devices (2 Corinthians 2:11).

We are called to be active in this world and to be the light, but not to be influenced by it.

WHAT ARE WE CALLED TO BE SEPARATED FROM?

Since we understand holiness is to be set apart or separated, the question is, what is God separating us from? If you read Galatians 5:19-21, you will find out some of the reasons why God wants us to be holy and be separated from this world. You see, in this world we have adultery, fornication, pornography, and all manners of sexual immoralities, and God wants His people to be separated from this moral defilement by being faithful to Him and obeying His words. The Lord wants us to be separated from everything unclean and indecent in the world by living righteously. God wants His people that are called by His name to depart from envy, strife, anger, idolatry, sorcery, enmity, jealousy, selfishness, divisiveness, a party spirit, drunkenness, carousing, and the likes of such iniquities. There has to be a difference between a child of God and an unbeliever.

If you are a parent and live in a gang-infested neighborhood, you will be right to caution your children not to be influenced by the gang activity around them. In the same way, God is calling us to live to influence this world but not be influenced by it.

He is calling you and me to live righteously and in holiness and to stop living like the world. We are to bear the fruit of His spirit as explained in Galatians 5:22-23, bearing the fruit of love, joy, peace, long-suffering, being gentle, and good to one another. We are to live like the children of the kingdom of God by being faithful to God. We must be gentle as a dove in meekness and humility, not be arrogant and proud but live a life of self-control not giving in to temptation and sin from the devil. All this may sound overwhelming but you are not the one doing the separation. The Holy Spirit that resides in you will give you the grace to live holy. You just have to genuinely desire to walk in holiness.

Don't be fooled by the lie of the devil that says you are human and subject to sin and cannot be holy. You are called by God who is able to empower you to live a holy life.

God cannot stand sin, He detests it. Moses saw that firsthand when he disobeyed God by striking the rock instead of speaking to it as God had commanded. As a result of that single disobedience, he was not allowed to set foot on the Promised Land. God is not a respecter of persons, and his laws apply to everyone. When you sin, you become a slave to satan because the Bible states we are slaves to whom we obey. satan is the author of disobedience and sin.

WHAT MUST I DO TO BE HOLY?

As children of God, we must hunger and thirst for righteousness (Matthew 5:6), but what must I do personally to be holy as God has commanded me? The fact that you are interested in this question indicates a level of hunger for a change, and according to Matthew 5:6, you are already blessed because you thirst and hunger after righteousness. May the Lord fill you in Jesus mighty name.

Our holiness or setting apart was instant when we gave our lives to the Lord and repented from our sins. So it was automatic as we were translated from the kingdom of darkness to the kingdom of light. 1 Peter 2:9 reminds us that we were chosen and set apart by God as a royal priesthood and as a holy nation. So holiness is not something we achieved by our works; it was God who chose to set us apart from the children of perdition. It is comforting to know that my holiness, my setting apart was by God, not my human effort.

WHAT MUST I DO TO MAINTAIN MY STATE OF HOLINESS?

1. REMAIN IN CHRIST JESUS

As illustrated earlier, if the children that lived in a gang-infested neighborhood somehow got themselves involved in a gang activity after their parents warned them not to, then they are no longer separated from the gang activity—they are now fully involved and have allowed the gang to influence them. Same way if we were separated by God as in holiness and later in life, we disobeyed God and got influenced with the filthy things of this world, then the logical and spiritual thing to do is to repent and retrace our steps back to God.

In Revelation 3, God wrote a letter to the church of Sardis warning them that He has not found their works perfect before Him. So God was saying to them, "I have something against you. Your lifestyle is not perfect before me, and there is something you are doing that I am not happy about." So God was telling them "begin now to retrace your steps and strengthen the good virtue that you have left" or He will come to them unexpectedly. So we must not be in spiritual slumber but be watchful, alert, and sober-minded for our adversary, the devil, goes about like a roaring lion seeking whom he may devour (1 Peter 5:8).

2. Yield to the Spirit of God

One of the keys to maintaining or strengthening our spiritual walk with God is to allow the Holy Spirit to lead us. The Bible tells us in Romans 8:14 that "for as many as are led by the Spirit of God, they are the sons of God." We can never go wrong when we are led by the Spirit of God.

The Spirit of God dwells in all believers, and He is there to direct our path and show us the right path to take. He is there to teach us all things and to counsel us in making the right decisions. So we must allow the Holy Spirit to lead us.

3. Fellowship with God in Prayer

The Bible admonishes us in Luke 18:1 that we ought to pray always and not faint. When we pray, we receive answers from God. Except we ask, and ask in accordance to the will of God, we are not entitled to receive (James 4:3). Prayer moves the hand of God in your life. Jesus always prayed to the Father while He was on earth, and if prayer is not important in the life of a believer, Christ would not have spent forty days and nights fasting and praying. When temptation came, He was well-equipped to say no to the wiles of the devil. So prayer will keep your mind spiritually tuned to God.

4. Read the Word of God Regularly

The Word of God is very important to keep the fire of God burning in us. The Lord has a word for us daily, but if you ask a majority of believers if the Lord speaks to them daily, they will probably say no because they do not equate reading the Word of God as the Lord talking to them. Most of the complicated equipment that are manufactured have manuals that explain why the equipment was manufactured and how to use it. Same way our God created us; He did not leave us like an orphan to go and figure it out ourselves. He gave us a manual called the Holy Bible. It is a book set apart from any other books, and it reveals to us many things we need to know such as who we are and what is our purpose in this world. The Word of God is light on our path; otherwise, we will be blind spiritually. So communing with God on a regularly basis is needed to maintain our state of holiness. We are not only to read the Word of God but to let the *rhema* Word of God speak to us. And most importantly, we must observe to do God's Word and allow the Holy Spirit to perfect everything concerning us.

SHOULD WE CONTINUE TO SIN HAVING KNOWN THE TRUTH?

Sin separates us from God, and it takes repentance to restore our right standing with God. But my question for you is, how long will you continue to repent for the same sin? God cannot be mocked. We cannot use His grace as an excuse to continue to sin knowing that He is always there to forgive us.

What then? Shall we sin because we are not under law but under grace? God forbid. Know ye not, that to whom ye yield yourselves servants to obey, his servants ye are to whom ye obey; whether of sin unto death, or of obedience unto righteousness

—Romans 6:15

God is a jealous God, and when you sin, you are making the evil one your master, and you become a slave to him—and that does not sit well with God. He is jealous of you and wants you as His child. The Lord has bought us with His precious blood and has set us free from darkness, out of bondage, and out of a life that was destined for hell. The Lord never ceases to be holy. He never put aside His holiness and played with sin. We must remain constantly in the state of holiness, and it is not something we put on only on Sundays but every moment of our lives. God hates sin and so should we.

The Bible talks about carnally minded versus spiritually minded Christians. Romans 8:1 says, "There is therefore now no condemnation to them which are in Christ Jesus, who walk not after the flesh, but after he Spirit." This scripture has been quoted many times, and most people that quote it always leave out part *b* of this Bible verse. They will say, "There is therefore now no condemnation to them which are in Christ Jesus," but they will conveniently leave out the part *b*, which is the qualifying part of that scripture. You see, for every promise of God, there is a condition to be met. If for example you want God's financial blessing, you have to sow a financial seed into the kingdom of God because it does not answer to prayer and fasting.

No farmer in his right mind will stay home and pray for harvest when he did not sow a seed in the ground. Same way for us to benefit from the promises of God, we must meet the condition set for the manifestation of that promise.

So when God says, "There is therefore now no condemnation to them which are in Christ Jesus, **who** walk not after the flesh, but after the Spirit."

This means that when we subscribe to the works of the flesh, that is allowing our emotions and bodily feelings to lead us to sin, we are subject to condemnation. However, when we subscribe to the spirit of truth which is the Holy Spirit to control our emotions, thoughts, and actions, then we are not subject to any form of condemnation. So to be exempt from condemnation, we must walk in the spirit, and when we do so, we cannot sin. The Bible states in Galatians 5:16, "This I say then, walk in the spirit and ye shall not fulfill the lust of the flesh." This is the essence in which this book was written. We must begin to wake up from our spiritual slumber and walk perfectly and blamelessly before God because His grace is sufficient.

Holiness, therefore, is a lifestyle, and one which every Christian should live effortlessly through the grace of God. It is not being busy as it pertains to religious activities. As we learned in Luke 10:38-42, Martha was very busy doing the religious activities; she was cooking and serving the Lord alone while her sister Mary sat at the feet of Jesus and did not move an inch. When Martha complained, she was surprised at the answer Jesus gave her. Jesus said in Luke 10:41-42, "Martha, Martha, thou art careful and troubled about many things: but one thing is needful: and Mary hath chosen that good part which shall not be taken away from her." Your works can be burnt to ashes or taken away from you if your motive is not right. But one thing you should seek to protect is your salvation and relationship with God. Guide it and work it out with fear and trembling (Philippians 2:12).

PURITY

WHY DO WE NEED PURITY IN OUR WALK WITH GOD?

Purity is defined by the *Holman Illustrated Bible Dictionary* as a "state of being or process of becoming free of inferior elements." Purity is a vital component in our walk with God. The Bible describe God's attribute as both holy and pure. He cannot stand an impure heart. Heaven is a holy place and nothing unholy will enter into it (Revelation 21:27). And in 2 Timothy 2:19, we are reminded that "nevertheless the foundation of God standeth sure, having this seal, The Lord knoweth them that are his. And, let everyone that nameth the name of Christ depart from iniquity."

We are called to purge ourselves from every form of iniquity so we can be presented before the Father as a vessel unto honor, sanctified, and fit for the Master's use.

> *If a man therefore purge himself from these, he shall be a vessel unto honour, sanctified, and meet for the master's use and prepared unto every good work. Flee also youthful lusts: but follow righteousness, faith, charity, peace, with them that call on the Lord out of a pure heart.*
>
> —2 Timothy 2:21-22

Heaven is going to be filled with people that love Jesus and have spiritually conformed to his image and likeness. These are holy people of God. The redeemed, of the Lord.

WHERE WILL YOU SPEND ETERNITY?

There comes a time in our lives, if we are not already there, that we begin to contemplate where we will spend eternity. We think about what to eat and what college to attend, what corporate job to apply for, what home to buy, and how much money to amass for retirement, but not very often do people ponder where they will spend eternity.

In Ecclesiastes, King Solomon lamented and discovered the vanity of this world. He discovered that the pleasure that the world offers is only temporary, and it leaves you empty. The pleasure of sins that the world offers is only temporal, and at the end, leads to death in hell. Read what King Solomon discovered.

I gathered me also silver and gold, and the peculiar treasure of kings and of the provinces: I gat me men singers and women singers, and the delights of the sons of men, as musical instruments, and that of all sorts.

So I was great, and increased more than all that were before me in Jerusalem: also my wisdom remained with me.

And whatsoever mine eyes desired I kept not from them, I withheld not my heart from any joy; for my heart rejoiced in all my labour: and this was my portion of all my labour.

Then I looked on all the works that my hands had wrought, and on the labour that I had laboured

to do: and, behold, all was vanity and vexation of spirit, and there was no profit under the sun."
—Ecclesiastes 2:8-11 (KJV)

King Solomon, one of the richest and wisest kings of his days, in an attempt to find lasting pleasure, acquired seven hundred wives and three hundred concubines to which the Lord already told the children of Israel not to marry strange women (1 King 11:1-3). He acquired all manners of material wealth in an attempt to quench his thirst for lasting joy. He failed. He discovered that all his attempts to find joy in material possessions was vanity upon vanity and futile. He realized that the world cannot offer anything permanent, whether it is riches, pleasure, happiness, joy, or peace. Only Jesus has the living water that will quench our thirst. He gives it freely to all who thirst for it. He concluded by saying in Ecclesiastes 12:13-14, "Let us hear the conclusion of the whole matter: Fear God and keep His commandments: for this is the whole duty of man. For God shall bring every work into judgment, with every secret thing, whether it be good, or whether it be evil."

King Solomon, with all his wisdom, concluded that the whole duty of man was to fear God and keep His commandments.

What Must I Do to Purify My Heart?

One way we can purify our hearts is by drawing near to the Lord and allowing him to cleanse our hearts from every evil thought. James 4:8 states, "Draw nigh to God, and he will draw nigh to you. Cleanse your hands, ye sinners; and purify your hearts, ye double minded."

Purifying your heart is a daily process. Our heart has to be pure toward God and our hands clean toward our neighbors on a daily basis. You don't know what day or hour the Lord will appear and take His church.

> *Blessed are the pure in heart for they shall see God.*
>
> —Matthew 5:8

It is only with a pure heart that you can see God. The Spirit of God cannot dwell in an unclean vessel. We must continue to shun evil and have the fear of God in our hearts. If we sin and come short, the Lord is faithful to forgive us if we confess our sins. We must not take his grace for granted.

Joseph spoke to Potiphar's wife in the book of Genesis 39:9, saying, "How then can I do this great wickedness, and sin against God?" Joseph had so much reverence and fear for God that he refused to sin against God. In the face of temptation, he chose to flee and not sin against God.

Can that be said of us? Do you have a nagging sin that is a thorn in your flesh—that sin that seems to cause you to stumble in your walk with God? It could be anger, envy, lust, idolatry. Whatever the sin is, give it to God for He alone is able to bring healing. God alone is able to restore a smoker, a drunkard, and a fornicator. There is no sickness the great physician cannot heal for His grace is truly sufficient. As Hebrews 12 reminds us, stating, "Wherefore seeing we also are compassed about with so great a cloud of witness, let us lay aside every weight, and the sin which doth so easily beset us, and let us run with patience the race that is set before us" (Hebrews 12:1).

So how do we lay to rest these sins that easily beset us? Our first response is to admit that we cannot handle it. We have to cry unto the Lord to give us grace to overcome the weight of sin. You are deceiving yourself if you think you can handle it yourself. Look up to Jesus Christ for help. Cast it upon Him for He is the author and finisher of our faith.

Chapter 7

Be Perfect

Growing up as a Christian, I have often heard people say and teach that we are not perfect and that we cannot attain perfection until we go to heaven. It has been preached in the pulpit and taught in Sunday schools. This is not biblical because God has clearly called His sons and daughters to a life of perfection.

> *Be ye therefore perfect even as your Father which is in heaven is perfect.*
> —Matthew 5:48

What Is the Bible's Definition of Perfection?

I like the way the Amplified Bible explained this verse.

You, therefore, must be perfect {growing into complete maturity of godliness in mind and character, having reached the proper height of virtue and integrity}, as your heavenly Father is perfect.

—Matthew 5:48

So what does it mean to walk in perfection? It simply means growing into complete maturity of godliness (holiness) in one's soul, which is the mind, will, and emotion. And this is what forms our characters and personalities. Man is a spirit; he has a soul, and he lives in a body. The instant you repented and gave your life to Jesus, you were made righteous and blameless in the sight of God in your spirit man, which is the real you (2 Corinthians 5:17-21). But your soul (mind, will, and emotion) has to be renewed to conform to the image and likeness of God. This is why the Bible constantly reminds us to renew our minds and to set our affections on things above, not things on the earth (Romans 12:2, Colossians 3:1-2, and Philippians 4:8). We have to constantly feed our minds with things that are true, things that are honest and just, things that are pure and lovely, and things that are of good report, virtues, or praise. We are to think about them. And as we do so, the Holy Spirit begins to help us to grow into complete maturity of godliness in mind and character, arming us with the strength required to reach the proper height of virtue and integrity—and that is perfection!

The Lord is calling us to a glorious and virtuous walk, and He has armed us with power to live a godly and perfect life with Him.

> *According as his divine power hath given unto us all things that pertain unto life and godliness, through the knowledge of him that hath called us to glory and virtue*
>
> —2 Peter 1:3

In practical terms, perfection means being God-like as you love your neighbors including your human foes, being God-like as you hate sin and shun evil, being God-like as you choose to do good rather than evil, and being God-like in exercising self-control. Read how my nine-year-old son Stephen defined perfection. He said, "Dad, perfection is like walking in God's footsteps." I could not have explained it any better. That is exactly what God wants from us. He is looking for a few believers that are willing to abandon their lives to follow Him. Those few that are willing to die to sin, die to self, and die to this world. Jesus told the rich young man, "If you want to be perfect, go sell all you have and give to the poor, and come follow me." In other words, lose your attachment to material things and worldly possessions; be dead to them and come take on Jesus. But the young man walked sorrowfully away from the one that would perfect him (Matthew 19:20-21). At no time did Jesus say to the rich young man, "You cannot be perfect or wait until you go to heaven then you will be made perfect." Rather Jesus told him, "If thou wilt be perfect, go and sell that thou hast, and give to the poor, and thou shalt have treasure in heaven and come and follow me" (Matthew 19:21).

This tells me that I can be made perfect if I receive and follow Jesus because as He is perfect, so am I in this world (1 John 4:17).

For by one offering he hath perfected forever them that are sanctified

—Hebrews 10:14

We the believers in Christ Jesus and the redeemed of God have been made holy, perfect, and sanctified by the offering of the blood of Jesus Christ. Read how Hebrews 10:10 Amp captured it: And in accordance with this will [of God], we have been made holy {consecrated and sanctified} through the offering made once for all of the body of Jesus Christ {the Anointed One}.

The battle for souls is being fought nowhere else but the mind. That is why Apostle Paul, in all seriousness, stated in Romans 12:1-2, "I beseech you therefore brethren." In other words, "I plead with you, brothers and sisters in Christ," and he continued by saying, "By the mercies of God, that ye present your bodies a living sacrifice, holy, acceptable unto God, which is your reasonable service. And be not conformed to this world: but be ye transformed by the renewing of your mind, that ye may prove what is that good, and acceptable, and perfect, will of God."

Your mind cannot be transformed to the perfect image of God until you renew it; likewise, your body cannot be transformed into the perfect likeness of the body of Jesus until you sacrifice it to God as a living sacrifice.

> *Mortify therefore your members which are upon the earth; fornication, uncleanness, inordinate affection, evil concupiscence, and covetousness, which is idolatry.*
>
> —Colossians 3:5

We have to put to death the sinful desires of our bodies, and this is the desire of God for every believer. He is waiting to grant you the grace to walk perfectly with Him. As the Spirit of God dwells within us, He begins to prune every dead works from us and perfect us into the image and likeness of God—no longer living in carnality but living by the dictate of the Spirit of God that dwells in you and me. Perfection means coming to full maturity in your spiritual walk with God, living virtuously for Christ and lacking nothing in your spiritual and moral character. It is the will of God that we take on His attributes. May God grant us the grace to live perfectly with Him.

SURRENDER COMPLETELY TO JESUS

Serving God requires singleness of mind and wholeness of heart. We cannot be double-minded when we serve God. Psalm 119:10 states, "With my whole heart have I sought thee: O let me not wander from thy commandments." It is apparent that God is calling His sons and daughters to return to their first love in Christ Jesus. We have been distracted by the values and cares of this world that the only time we give God our complete attention is during a few hours on Sundays. May the Lord forgive us in Jesus name.

Thou shalt be perfect with the Lord thy God.
—Deuteronomy 18:13

We are clearly called to live a life that is perfect and blameless before God, not giving the devil cause to accuse us before our Heavenly Father. Our conduct as Christians or followers of Christ reflects positively or negatively on God. Every father wants honor, not dishonor, from their children, and our God is no different. Romans 2:24 states, "For the name of God is blasphemed among the Gentiles through you, as it is written."

People are watching how you live in your private or public life, and your conduct and character reflect on God. When we identify ourselves as children of God, and we do something unbecoming of children of God, believers and unbelievers alike may say, "Wow, and he calls himself a Christian and a child of God?" This brings reproach to our Heavenly Father and makes unbelievers blaspheme His holy name.

Living under grace does not give us permission to live as the world lives. Rather, the grace of God should make us sober-minded in loving God even more with all our hearts, our souls, and our might (Deuteronomy 6:5). The grace of God should make us reflect on God's goodness to the extent we would not want to be the cause of God's name being blasphemed by unbelievers. May His grace cause us to be a channel of His love and light in this dark world.

Our spiritual perfection comes not from the east or west but from the work Christ did on the cross. Through our rebirth in Christ Jesus, we receive righteousness—no longer slaves to sin but sons and daughters of the Most High God. We are no longer under the influence of our flesh but led by the Spirit of God, which is the spirit of excellence. Everything God created was good and perfect, and as we are led by His Spirit, we begin to experience and exhibit His image, His likeness, and His perfection.

How can we confidently present ourselves before God if we are living in anger, jealousy, strife, malice, and immorality? It is only when we turn and repent from our wicked and sinful ways and choose to live a life free from every form of immoral defilement that we can boldly stand on the day of judgment. We must never forget that our boldness is not based on confidence in our flesh; rather, confidence on the grace God gave us to live a godly life. As He is, so must we be in this world.

Every decision we make in life is based on choice. We have a choice regardless of the circumstances in which we grew up—the choice to excel in life or to live a mediocre life. There are documented proofs of children born in the slum rising to greater heights in life. So we cannot stand before God and tell Him the reason we did not serve Him and live a godly, fruitful life is because of our family situation. God already knew our family situation before He formed us in our mother's wombs. That is the reason He sent us there so we can be the light and salt in our family. He did not save us so we can wallow in self-pity. Rather, He saved us so that we can be children of destiny. We are the ones that are fearfully and wonderfully made in the image and likeness of God. Nothing poor or substandard can be attributed to our creation because our God is not substandard. He is an excellent God.

When it came to creating man, the Godhead, which consists of the Father, Son, and Holy Spirit, were present, and they had a conference and agreed to create man totally different from any of their other creations including angels, plants, and animals. They agreed that man will be created in their image and likeness (Genesis 1:26). And not only that, man will be created a little lower than God, and in addition, man will be crowned with glory and honor. In essence, God made man as the second in command only to Him. He gave us dominion over His creations, including His heavenly hosts and those fallen angels.

That is how valuable you are to God. Also, as you know, God spoke into existence His other creations, but when it came to man, God rolled up His sleeves and got His hands dirty for humanity by creating man out of clay. What an awesome God that loves us so much. David wrote in Psalm

8:4, "What is man, that thou are mindful of him? And the son of man, that thou visited him?" What a privilege to be created in the image and likeness of God.

He confers on us dominion over all His creation on earth. What that means is that we do not have to beg for food, it is ours (Psalm 37:25); we do not have to beg for that job, it is ours (Psalm 24:1). You do not have to fear starting that business the Lord has laid in your heart, it is your covenant right to be employer of labor. That is your covenant right as a born-again believer who is living in righteousness.

Your spirit, which is the real you, has been made perfect in this world. The Bible says as Jesus is, so are we in this world (1 John 4:17). So if Christ is love, then I am love; if Christ is righteous, then I am righteous; if Christ is perfect and without sin, so I am perfect and without sin. When you repented and gave your life to Jesus, He wiped away every sin you ever committed and made you righteous (2 Corinthians 5:21).

TRUST IN JESUS, NOT YOUR POSSESSIONS

Then said Jesus unto his disciples, Verily I say unto you, That a rich man shall hardly enter into the kingdom of heaven. And again I say unto you, It is easier for a camel to go through the eye of a needle, than for a rich man to enter into the kingdom of God.

When the disciples heard it, they were exceedingly amazed, saying, who then can be saved? But Jesus beheld them, and said unto them, with men this is impossible; but with God all things are possible.

—Matthew 19:23-26

There was only one thing the rich young man was missing to be perfect. He was missing Jesus Christ. He walked away from the one person that will make him perfect.

When you come to a fork on the road, what decision would you make? The rich young man came to that fork and chose to keep his earthly possessions rather than commit to Jesus. The rich young man was trusting in himself to make it to heaven. He was trusting in his obedience of the law instead of the grace of our Lord Jesus Christ. Like most unbelievers, the rich young man was trusting in his abilities rather than the free grace of God.

He was sad and sorrowful when Jesus asked him to sell his possessions and give to the poor. What lesson can we learn from the story of this rich young man's encounter with Christ?

First, we learned that we cannot depend on our strength or our works to enter into the kingdom of God.

Secondly, when we give our time, talents, and treasure for the kingdom's sake, we are laying up treasures in heaven for ourselves. We can never outgive God; as we give to His kingdom, we receive the harvest here on earth and the reward in heaven. So it is always a win-win situation when we give to the Lord cheerfully. This is what the rich young man failed to realize. We came to this world with nothing, and we will depart with nothing. We must loosen our grip on material things and focus on what is eternal.

Thirdly, in verse 25 of Matthew 19, the disciples were quoted as saying, "Who then can be saved?" and Jesus replied, saying, "With men this is impossible; but with God all things are possible."

To live a life of perfection outside of Christ is impossible, and it is only by the grace of God that impossibilities can turn to possibilities.

> *For the Law never made anything perfect but the bringing in of a better hope did; by the which we draw nigh unto God.*
>
> —Hebrews 7:19

Your perfection does not come from you keeping the law just like the rich young man found out. He did everything in his power to keep the law but still fell short. Just like most of us, we are relying on our works to make heaven or attain perfection. Jesus perfected us, and in the eyes of our Heavenly Father, we are sanctified and righteous and without sin.

THE WAY, THE TRUTH, AND THE LIFE

Jesus declared in John 14:6 that "I am the way, the truth, and the life: no man cometh unto the Father, but by me." The way to salvation does not lie with the world but through Jesus Christ. Likewise, the truth does not lie in the world but in Jesus Christ. And when you receive Jesus as your Lord and Savior, you receive a life-changing truth through the power of the Holy Spirit that sets you free from the clutches of satan.

> *Howbeit when he, the Spirit of truth, is come, he*
> *will guide you into all truth: for he shall not speak*
> *of himself; but whatsoever he shall hear, that shall*
> *he speak: and he shall shew you things to come.*
> —John 16:13

> *And ye shall know the truth, and the truth shall*
> *make you free.*
> —John 8:32

The truth of the saving grace of God is what set me free from the clutches of satan and the bondage of sin. That same truth can set you free from all your addictions and sinful desires. The Bible says in John 8:36, "If the son therefore shall make you free, ye shall be free indeed."

You see, the world thinks that the more knowledge they acquire, that translates to having authority over the truth. The world relies on scientists to prove that God does not exist, but their wisdom is foolishness in the sight of God (1 Corinthians 3:19). They have acquired all this knowledge but are still blind to the truth. The revelation of Jesus Christ comes beyond head knowledge, and it takes the revelatory work of the Holy Spirit to know the truth.

It is the will of God that those who are called by His name separate themselves from this world and live a life of integrity and a life worthy of our repentance (Matthew 3:8). Integrity is synonymous with honesty, truthfulness, honor, reliability, and uprightness. We are called to live a life of these desirable qualities, and Jesus is the way to achieve it.

You Are Armed with Grace for Perfection

Any work you do on your own without the grace of God is like a filthy rag before God. Our hope for perfection comes not from our own power in keeping the law but through what Christ did for us on the cross. Until you realize that and surrender every area of your life to Jesus, you will walk away sorrowfully like the rich young man. May that not be your portion in Jesus name.

The Bible tells us in Galatians 5:16-18 that there is a war between our flesh and spirit, and as a result, we are not able to do those things that we ought to do. Because of this great war, we are not able to make a spiritually mature decision. No wonder we still struggle as believers at times. Though we say we are born again and Holy Spirit-filled, our actions at times do not bring glory to God. Some believers still struggle with anger, unforgiveness, lust, and immorality, which are all the work of the flesh. We cannot win this war on our own strength. We need the power of the Most High God to break the yoke of the enemy, and we need the grace of God to walk perfectly with Him.

> *God is my strength and power: and he maketh*
> *my way perfect.*
> —2 Samuel 22:33

If we are to work perfectly with God, we must choose to put an end to the war that is raging between the spirit and the flesh, and the Holy Spirit will give you the grace if you so desire. A dead person cannot commit adultery, and a dead person cannot sin. That is why the Bible encourages us in 1 Corinthians 9:27 to make no provision for the flesh; rather, to bring our body under subjection so as to allow the new man, which is your born-again Spirit and the real you, to live a godly life.

Ask the Holy Spirit to take absolute control of your life and take control of every decision you will make and every thought that occupies your mind. The moment you yield yourself to the Spirit of God, the raging war between the spirit and the flesh terminates. The Spirit of God takes over and becomes the driver of your life.

When you were a baby, you acted like a baby; and when you grew up, you gave up childish behaviors. So God is calling us to a higher level of spiritual relationship. He wants us to grow up in our walk with Him. As a babe and new convert, it is understandable that you spoke, understood, walked, and acted like a child. God's expectation is that as we grow in the knowledge and understanding of Him, our actions, our walk, and our relationship with Him should reflect our spiritual maturity. No parents will be happy to see their eighteen-year-old son still in a diaper, crawling on all four extremities instead of walking upright. Same way, God is not pleased when we are still speaking like a child and acting like a child. Do your daily walk and actions reflect maturity in your Christian walk, or is it only on Sundays or midweek services that people know you are a Christian? The Lord is calling us to a life of perfection, a life of spiritual maturity. He wants you to reach the proper height of virtue and integrity in your walk with Him. Christianity is not a cloak that you put on and take off at your convenience. As a follower of Christ, it is your way of life. Your character and the image you portray to others in your workplace or in public reflect on your Heavenly Father who is watching your every move.

When our decisions are not in line with the Word of God, then we are spiritually immature. For example, we are spiritually immature when we choose to disobey God and practice loving only those that love us, knowing fully well that the Lord commanded us in His words in Luke 6:27-28 to also love our enemies, to do good to them who hate us, to bless them that curse us, and to pray for them who despitefully use us. Spiritual maturity means making a decisive choice to obey God rather than allowing the lust of our flesh to be fulfilled. Abraham made a decisive choice to obey God and would have sacrificed his only son, Isaac, if God had not intervened. It means choosing to render mercy and forgiveness to someone that has rightly wronged you. It also means choosing not to partake of immoral acts when you have every opportunity to do so. We cannot be spiritually perfect on our own. Certainly, we have a role to play. The Bible says in Psalm 18:32 that "it is God who arms me with strength, and makes my way perfect." One thing God will never do is force His will on us. This was evident in Jesus encounter with the rich young man. At no time did Jesus force him to obey His instructions. Likewise, our role starts with yearning to live a life of perfection. We have to first desire to live righteously for God, and it starts with having the Spirit of the fear of the Lord. This spirit has kept me on a straight path with God and has delivered me from diverse temptations common to man. If you sincerely desire this Spirit, ask the Holy Spirit to baptize you with the spirit of the fear of the Lord.

The next step is to open your heart to God, allowing him to make the spiritual change that would make us conform to the image of God. It means renewing our minds daily to conform to the mind of Christ. Just like a parent guides and watches over his baby learning to walk, so will God guide and watch over you until your walk with Him is perfect. He will pick you up when you stumble and guide you through a way of escape when you are tempted. God will raise a standard when the adversary comes in like a flood, for this is His desire for you (Isaiah 59:19). The Lord has given us the way of escape over sin, and it is up to us to choose to walk in the Spirit. His Word says if we walk in the spirit, we will not fulfill the lust of the flesh (Galatians 5:16).

God clearly hates sin, and He turned away from Jesus in a split moment as Christ hung on the cross laden with the sin of the world (Matthew 27: 46). One who knew no sin was made to bear the sins of the world. It is through the work of Christ on the cross that we are made righteous and presented spotless and perfect before God the Father. The last words from Christ on the cross was "It is finished" (John 19:30). Christ took our sin when He died on the cross so that we may have abundant life with the Father. John declared when he saw Jesus, "Behold the Lamb of God which taketh away the sin of the world" (John 1:29).

We deny the work of Christ on the cross if we insist that we are still sinners and imperfect in the sight of God. As someone that has repented and is born again, you are no longer a habitual sinner but one that was saved by grace, one cleansed and made perfect and spotless by the blood of Jesus.

There is therefore now no condemnation to them which are in Christ Jesus, who walk not after the flesh, but after the Spirit.

—Romans 8:1

Living in the flesh brings nothing but death and condemnation. This is not our portion. Jesus is calling us to a life of spiritual maturity where the desires of our flesh are mortified. God is calling us to a life of holiness and purity where sin no longer rules us. For we have been bought with the precious blood of our Lord Jesus Christ. Invite the Holy Spirit today to come into your life and arm you with strength and power to walk a life of perfection and a life of holiness.

MAKE YOUR CHOICE TODAY

God does not want robots as sons and daughters. It is your choice to accept or reject Him, and He will draw near to you if you draw near to Him. However, there is a choice to make. Either you are for Christ wholeheartedly or you are for the world and the devil. The choice is yours. I have made my choice, and as for me and my household we will serve the Lord all the days of our lives. You cannot love the things of this world and still love God. The Bible states in 1 John 2:15, "Love not the world, neither the things that are in the world. If any man loves the world, the love of the father is not in him." The rich young man made his choice. What is your choice today? There is no middle way or bystanders in the battle between forces of good and of evil. If you are not for Christ, then you belong to the enemy's camp. Choose today whom you will serve, and I implore you to serve the living God that you and your household may live.

Behold, I stand at the door, and knock: if any man hear my voice, and open the door, I will come in to him, and will sup with him, and he with me.

—Revelation 3:20

Our life is filled with choices, and the choices we make will determine our destination. Adam had a choice to eat or not eat the forbidden fruit. He chose to eat the forbidden fruit and disobey God, and he paid for his disobedience. Abraham had a choice to either obey God and sacrifice His only son or spare the life of his only child and disobey God. He chose to obey God, and because of his obedient act, God declared in Genesis 22:17 that in blessing, He will bless Abraham; and in multiplying, He will multiply Abraham's seed as the stars of heaven.

Joseph also had a choice to make, to either sleep with Potiphar's wife or refuse to defile his body and sin against God. After all, Joseph was a handsome and vibrant young man in the prime of his life. But he chose to fear God and obey Him. He declared in Genesis 39:9, saying, "How then can I do this great wickedness, and sin against God." I love that. His act of obedience resulted in Joseph occupying the second-highest position in the land of Egypt. Even the angels of God are not created to be robots. They also have a choice to serve God or not. One-third of the angels decided to fall away with satan. The angels' act of disobedience sealed their eventual destination of hellfire. You don't have to end up with them, God has made a provision for your redemption. The Lord is asking you today to choose life and not death.

> *I call heaven and earth to record this day against you, that I have set before you life and death, blessing and cursing: therefore choose life, that both thou and thy seed may live:*
>
> —Deuteronomy 30:19

One Thing God Cannot Stand

There is one thing God cannot stand, and it is sin. He did not put up with it in Genesis, and He will not put up with it in Revelation. The Bible says in 1 Corinthians 6:9-10 (AMP),

> *Do you not know that the unrighteous and the wrongdoers will not inherit or have any share in the kingdom of God? Do not be deceived {misled}: neither the impure and immoral, nor idolaters, nor adulterers, nor those who participate*

in homosexuality, nor cheats {swindlers and thieves} nor greedy graspers, nor drunkards, nor foulmouthed revilers and slanderers, nor extortioners and robbers will inherit or have any share in the kingdom of God.

The Lord is desiring to replace your hatred with love, your sadness with joy, your anxiety with peace, your intolerance and anger toward people with long-suffering, your harshness with gentleness, and your evil deeds toward others with goodness. The Lord wants you to cast out your unbelief and take up faith in His saving grace. He wants you to shed a life of pride and take on His meekness. The Lord desires to corral your life that is spinning out of control and replace it with a life of temperance and self-control. Will you open your heart to Him today?

He wants to perfect us before His return, a church that is spotless and without wrinkles. Will you be one of the wise virgins today or the unwise ones? The hour is now, and the day is today. Don't put it off any longer for the bridegroom cometh like a thief in the night when you least expect Him.

He that overcomes shall inherit all things; and I will be his God, and he shall be my son. But the fearful, and unbelieving, and the abominable, and murderers, and whoremongers, and sorcerers, and idolaters, and all liars, shall have their part in the lake which burneth with fire and brimstone: which is the second death.

—Revelation 21:7-8

There is an overcoming of sin required for all believers, and Jesus did not leave you as an orphan. He gave you the Holy Spirit to be your helper. Will you cry to Him today? He is waiting and will not force His will on you.

A MAN THAT LIVED PERFECTLY FOR GOD

Many would say that it is not easy for us to live a perfect life, and they will rationalize it by saying we are human and bound to sin. But I have news for you today. There are people that lived perfectly for God in an era when grace did not abound. One of such persons is Job. Let us examine a few of them.

Now there was a day when the sons of God came to present themselves before the LORD, and satan came also among them. And the LORD said unto satan, whence comest thou? Then satan answered the Lord, and said, From going to and fro

*in the earth, and from walking up and down in it.
And the Lord said unto satan, Hast thou considered
my servant job, that there is none like him in the
earth, a **perfect** and an **upright man**, one that
feareth God and escheweth evil?*

—Job 1:6-8

If a man named Job walked perfectly before God in an
era when grace did not abound as we freely have it today
through the death of Christ on the cross, how much more
now that the Lord, through His grace, has armed us with
strength and made our way perfect? God is calling you out
from a life of imperfection to a life of a perfect walk with
Him. I rebuke every demonic stronghold that is keeping you
from living a perfect, holy, and upright life with God. You
shall fear God and seek after His holiness and purity in Jesus
mighty name. Let there be no doubt in your heart that you
too can live perfectly and upright for God just as Job did.
You have the creator of the universe in your corner, and He
promised you that He will never leave nor forsake you; and
above all, He has armed you with strength and made your
way perfect. Receive the grace now to stand firm and strong
over temptations and to shun evil. Receive the grace to say
yes to holiness and no to filthiness.

Let us examine what Job did to earn him the title of a perfect man in the eyes of God. Why did God declare his servant, Job, out of all the inhabitants of the earth, a perfect and upright man? God gave us the answer in the same verse. God calls Job "one that fears God, and eschews evil." The Bible tells us in Hebrews 13:8 that we serve a God that changes not for He is the same yesterday, today, and forever.

Job loved God, and because of his love for God, he feared God. To fear God is to shun evil.

> *The fear of the LORD is to hate evil: pride, and arrogancy, and the evil way, and the froward mouth, do I hate.*
>
> —Proverbs 8:13

Does the fear of God reign in your heart today, or are your feet too quick to run to sin on the pretense that we are human and bound to sin? That is the lie of the devil. You can live a sinless life with the grace of God. Let us turn away today from our destructive path and make a decision to live totally for God. No longer can we rest on the excuse that we are not perfect. God will not call you to do what He has not equipped you to do; otherwise, He will be an unfair God. But our God is fair and just for He has given you everything you need to live virtuously for Him. God is calling us to a life of moral excellence. Don't settle for lower standards. We serve a great and mighty God; let us not take His love for granted. The Bible asked, "Shall we continue to sin that grace may abound?" If the answer is no, let us then turn from our wicked ways and live for Him alone.

NOAH

In a world filled with corruption and violence, Noah found grace in the eyes of the Lord. Noah chose to live differently from the world. He lived to please God, not his fleshy desires. In Noah's days, men were lovers of themselves instead of lovers of God. Just like in our modern era, men are more interested in doing what is pleasing to them than what is pleasing to God. They are blind by their lust and prefer to live in the kingdom of darkness than living to please God. But Noah was righteous in the midst of unrepentant and rebellious people. He was faithful to God and walked blamelessly in the sight of God. The Bible said in Genesis 6:9, "Noah was a just man and perfect in his generations, and Noah walked with God." And the Bible tells us in verse 22 that Noah obeyed the Lord and did according to all that the Lord commanded. This is what separated Noah from the men of his generation. He loved the Lord enough to obey him. What a pleasure it is to walk perfectly with the

Lord. So you too can find grace in the sight of God to live a blameless and perfect walk with God.

ABRAHAM

Everyone God called, He called them to walk perfect with Him (Matthew 5:48), and Abraham was not an exception. In Genesis 17:1, we hear the Lord calling Abraham to a perfect walk with him.

> *And when Abram was ninety years old and nine, the Lord appeared to Abram, and said unto him, I am the Almighty God; walk before me, and be thou perfect.*
>
> —Genesis 17:1

Abraham believed God, and he showed it by the faith he had in God; and that pleased God for without faith, we cannot please the Lord (Hebrews 11:6).

Let us answer the call of Jesus and live perfectly for God. Let us have a healthy reverence and fear of God. Let us show Him that we love Him by living in obedience and shunning evil. Let us live in the spirit so we don't fulfill the desire of our flesh. May God give us the grace to live perfectly for Him in Jesus name.

God Is the Standard in Our High Calling

Whom are you measuring your spiritual maturity against? Is it your pastor, parent, spouse, or a well-known man or woman of God? In Philippians 3:11-13, Paul states that he counts himself as not having achieved perfection yet, but that he is forgetting things that are in the past and focusing on striving toward the mark of perfection. And in verse 15, he says, "Let as many as are spiritually perfect be thus minded."

Apostle Paul did great things for the kingdom of God. He wrote almost half of the New Testament and suffered greatly for the kingdom's sake, yet he is not our standard. We do not measure our spiritual walk with any man. You have been called to a life of moral excellence, a life of perfection, and your only standard is God. Call on Jesus today to give you power over sin.

Ability to live a life of perfection comes not from the east or west or from your hard work for they are like filthy rags before God. Perfection comes when you allow the great potter to produce a great masterpiece with your life. He will mold you from one that loves sin to one that detests sin. He will take your heart of stone and mold it into a heart of flesh, and He will take that disobedient heart and mold it into a heart that is in complete obedience to God. The Holy Spirit is waiting to perfect you.

IF WE OFFEND NOT IN WORDS, WE ARE PERFECT

Jesus is waiting to transform your life through the work of the Holy Spirit. Your tongue is a powerful weapon. We can choose to use our tongues to bless someone or to curse them. The tongue can build up and comfort someone or destroy and tear down someone. The tongue can bring joy to the depressed and healing to the sick. So the choice is ours.

> *For in many things we offend all. If any man offend not in word, the same is a perfect man, and able also to bridle the whole body.*
>
> —James 3:2

Choose to bridle your tongue, for if you offend not in word, you are a perfect man. God of light wants to transform you from darkness to the light of the world. He wants you to submit to Him and allow Him to be your shepherd.

> *A good man out of the good treasure of his heart bringeth forth that which is good; and an evil man out of the evil treasure of his heart bringeth forth*

that which is evil: for of the abundance of the heart his mouth speaketh.

—Luke 6:45

Can an orange seed produce a lemon tree? I believe the answer is no. Likewise, a born-again believer should not be found lying, slandering, gossiping, belittling, rude, harsh, or betraying. How can evil words come out of one that is good? Can light and darkness coexist? According to the above scripture, only an evil heart is capable of producing evil words. That tells me that whatever comes out of my mouth says a lot about the state or condition of my heart. So if I judge myself and find out that I still enjoy lying, gossiping, and the likes, then I must repent and ask the Holy Spirit to create in me a clean heart and renew a right spirit within me (Psalm 51:10).

WHY DON'T WE DESIRE TO BE PERFECT?

We all strive for excellence in every other area of our lives. Olympians live a life of many years of dedication and training, even denying themselves certain pleasures of life for a singular focus to win a medal that will perish. But when it comes to our Christian walk or a life without sin, we change our tune and say it is not possible to live a perfect life, or that it is not possible to live a life without sin. Yes, it is true you cannot live a holy life on your own, but with the grace of God, you can live a life without sin. You have to be willing to be pruned by the Holy Spirit. He can transform your life of bitterness and hatred to a life of joy and love. He can transform a life of depression to a life of hope in Christ Jesus, and He can transform a life of promiscuity to a life of self-control. If an Olympian can dedicate himself or herself into his or her sport, you as a believer and Holy Spirit-filled born-again can do even greater. You can surrender all that lust, hatred, anger, witchcraft, idolatry, and all those lies at the feet of Jesus, and take up His righteousness and perfection.

Why then do we feel it is impossible to live a life of perfection as the Lord has called us to live? Basically, it comes down to the lie of the devil. He is the father of lies and a master at that. Many in the church have bought the lie, and many have been deceived to think that spiritual perfection is unattainable and can only be attained in heaven and not on earth. Many give the excuse that we are human and bound to err. If we assume that, we make God a liar who has called you and me to a life of perfection (Matthew 5:48).

And that, knowing the time, that now it is high
time to awake out of sleep: for now is our salvation
nearer than when we believed.

The night is far spent, the day is at hand: let us therefore cast off the works of darkness, and let us put on the armour of light.

Let us walk honestly as in the day; not in rioting and drunkenness, not in chambering and wantonness, not in strife and envying.

But put you on the lord Jesus Christ, and make not provision for the flesh, to fulfill the lusts thereof.

—Romans 13:11-14

The time is now to wake up from our spiritual slumber and be ready like the five wise virgins. Jesus is coming when you least expect it. We are to be watchful so we are not found lacking. Let us therefore walk honestly with each other, not in strife and envy, not in sensuality and licentiousness nor in quarreling and jealousy as explained in the amplified version of the Bible, but rather by putting on the armor of light, clothing ourselves with the Lord Jesus Christ our Savior and making no provision for the flesh.

FINAL THOUGHT

I leave you with this farewell message from Paul, written essentially for us all.

Finally brethren, farewell. Be perfect, be of good comfort, be of one mind, live in peace; and the God of love and peace shall be with you.

—2 Corinthians 13:11

Paul's farewell message encouraging believers to be perfect—in other words, to live a life that is blameless before the Lord. He is calling us to be of good comfort and one mind with Christ, and to live peaceably with all men knowing that our God of love and peace is always with us. Let the peace of God be your guide as you walk perfectly with Him. God bless you!